C0-AKV-046

CHRISTIAN LIVES

The aim of this small collection of new biographies is to study outstanding Christians of the modern era, particularly some who have taken a lead in the ecumenical renewal of the Church in mission and unity. Thus a publishing venture may show some of the meaning of the words of Jesus: 'I have called you friends.'

Zinzendorf the Ecumenical Pioneer by A. J. Lewis is published simultaneously with *A Man To Be Reckoned With. African Saint: The Story of Apolo* by Anne Luck and *Paul Courturier and Christian Unity* by Geoffrey Curtis are in preparation.

A MAN TO BE
RECKONED WITH

WERNER HÜHNE

A MAN TO BE RECKONED WITH

The Story of
Reinold von Thadden-Trieglaff

Edited with a
Preface and Epilogue
by Mark Gibbs

SCM PRESS LTD
BLOOMSBURY STREET LONDON

Translated by Robert W. Fenn from
Reinold von Thadden-Trieglaff
by Werner Hühne
published by Kreuz Verlag, Stuttgart

This English language edition
has been edited by Mark Gibbs

FIRST PUBLISHED 1962

PRINTED IN GREAT BRITAIN BY
W. & J. MACKAY & CO LTD, CHATHAM

CONTENTS

ILLUSTRATIONS

PREFACE

This is the story of a great man and a great Christian. Reinold von Thadden-Trieglaff, Pomeranian landowner, army officer, student leader, founder of the Kirchentag Movement of the Christian laity, is famous enough in his own Germany but hardly more than a name in Britain and the United States. Yet is there any man alive with quite the same record?

As a young man he refused to fight a duel of honour, and was saved from disgrace in the army of 1914 only by the personal intervention of the Kaiser, William II. Between the wars he combined influential work for the students of Germany with a relentless opposition to Hitler, and was twice arrested by the Gestapo. During the Second World War, he held the senior position in the German army's occupation of Louvain—and after the war received the official thanks of the city for the humane way in which he carried out his duties. Refusing offers of asylum, in 1945 he returned to his Pomeranian estates, and on the arrival of the Soviet troops was promptly deported to prison camps in the Arctic circle. In 1946 he returned to Berlin, a ragged POW with his health and voice apparently ruined—and by 1949 he was the director of the greatest religious movement in modern Europe. In 1961 he calmly organized a church conference of 40,000 people in the crisis city of Berlin, and one of the major themes of this *Kirchentag*, in the year of the Eichmann trial, was 'Jews and Christians'.

Substantially, this book is a translation by Mr Robert Fenn from the original text by Dr Werner Hühne. It has, however, been freely adapted, and a concluding chapter added on the story down to the end of 1961. I should like to express my personal gratitude to Dr von Thadden-Trieglaff for his constant encouragement and help; and to Dr Hühne and the original publishers, Kreuz Verlag, for their most generous co-operation in permitting me to prepare this English edition.

An authoritative biography must wait until the subject's active life is done. This book is different: it is an introduction to the living man.

MARK GIBBS

A NOTE ON GERMAN CHURCH TERMINOLOGY

Evangelisch

Sometimes confusions arise over the word *Evangelische*, which means Protestant rather than 'Evangelical' in the Anglo-American sense. In Germany most people are *Evangelisch* or *Katholisch*, i.e. Protestant or Roman Catholic. But a man who is *Evangelisch* or Protestant may well belong to a Lutheran Church which is distinctly 'high church' in its worship and theology, so that even the word Protestant carries overtones in English which do not quite fit *Evangelisch*.

The German Evangelical Church, or *Evangelische Kirche in Deutschland*, is a federation of different *Landeskirchen*, or Provincial churches, which vary quite considerably in their style of worship.

Akademie

The *Evangelische Akademien* or 'Evangelical Academies' are *not* pietist secondary schools! They are centres for lay training, of which the first and most famous is the one at Bad Boll, near Stuttgart. They have been called 'academies' in the original, Platonic, sense of being places for free discussion and argument.

Kirchentag[1]

Literally 'Church Day', and so used in various contexts in the nineteenth century. Sometimes translated Church Rally or Church Congress. Thadden adopted this name for his movement partly to link up with the ninteenth-century tradition of big meetings for lay people. In this book the word is used both of the special rallies and of the organization linking them.

Normally a modern Kirchentag lasts for more than one day. It starts on a Wednesday, and some 40,000 people enrol for the whole programme of lectures, Bible studies, and discussion groups. It ends with a large open-air rally on the Sunday afternoon, the *Hauptversammlung*—with anything up to 650,000 present, according to circumstances.

[1] See *Meet the Church*, a booklet about the Kirchentag published by the World Council of Churches, Geneva.

The Confessional Church, or *Bekkennende Kirche*

The secret underground Protestant Church which opposed the Nazification of the official Protestant bodies. The translation 'Confessing Church' is often preferred. See E. H. Robertson, *Christians against Hitler*, SCM Press 1962.

M.G.

I

IN THE KAISER'S ARMY

THE Thaddens come from the territory once belonging to the Dukes of Pomerania-Danzig in the area of East Germany colonized by the Teutonic Order in the Middle Ages. They are of Slav origin, and the family can be traced back to a knight whose Christian name was Tadeusz, and who was born about 1270. The family soon spread into the district of Lauenburg-Bütow, and the village of Thadden (Polish Tadzino) not far from Lake Zarnowitz derives its name from them.

The Thaddens have been local squires rather than national figures, serving faithfully enough in the Prussian and German armies, good landlords and local magistrates, but without great importance in the history books. One of them, Adolf Ferdinand von Thadden (who was the first to take over the estate at Trieglaff in Pomerania), is notable both as a friend of Bismarck's and also as a leader of the evangelical revival in Pomerania in the 1820s and '30s.

Although Reinold von Thadden likes to call himself 'a simple countryman', he did not, strictly speaking, come from the country at all. His childhood and early youth were spent mainly in small towns. He was born on 13th August, 1891, at Mohrungen in East Prussia, and he attended grammar schools at Greifenberg and in Brandenburg. He went to live permanently in the country in 1921, when he was thirty years old, and took over his father's estate at Vahnerow.

His father, Adolf von Thadden, was a civil lawyer. At the time when his only son was born he was provincial governor at Mohrungen. Later he was transferred to Greifenberg in his native

Pomerania and when he took over the old family estate of Trieglaff he continued as Governor at Greifenberg.

Reinold's father was a tall, handsome man, quiet and contemplative by nature rather than active and enterprising. The few surviving friends who once enjoyed his hospitality at Trieglaff and Greifenberg remember his simple piety, his great charm and his artistic tastes. In summer he liked to take part in theatrical performances occasionally in the park. He left the management of his estates mainly to his stewards. He could do this without anxiety, since the serious crisis that had threatened German agriculture in the 1890s had passed. The rapid transition of Germany from an agrarian to an industrial state had led to a catastrophic slump in the price of agricultural products. A series of bad harvests, a flood of cheap imported grain from America and Russia, the competition of imported wool from Australia and South Africa, combined to bring about the breaking up of very many large estates. But tariffs were soon imposed on imported agricultural products; so that German agriculture enjoyed a comparatively favourable position until 1914, and the Thadden estates prospered.

In Greifenberg, where he was Governor for thirty years, Adolf von Thadden was highly respected. He had a passion for hunting and whenever he drove through the neighbourhood in his coach he always carried his gun. His hobby was trees, and he had a high reputation among arboriculturalists and carried on a correspondence with many of them and with landscape gardeners. He was often able to provide budget grants for roadside trees; with one exception—the main road from Trieglaff to Greifenberg along which he travelled in his coach every day was relegated to the end of the queue in order to avoid any suspicion that he was making use of public funds for his own advantage. That was in the best tradition of Pomeranian officials.

Such was Reinold von Thadden's father, a prosperous landowner and a conscientious official, a sociable man with many interests, always sincerely concerned for the welfare of his people, and holding to the Christian tradition of his family—but also a man of easy-going temperament, inclined to avoid any deep and serious personal involvement. He was much too happy-go-lucky to be able to sympathize fully with the serious, brooding temperament of his son.

Reinold's mother was the daughter of an officer in the Royal Prussian Guards. She was a Gerlach, a family prominent in Berlin government circles in the nineteenth century, with a strong tradition of interest in religious and social work. For instance, her grandfather, Otto von Gerlach, a Protestant minister, had set up a work centre for unemployed weavers in Berlin. She died when Reinold was only eighteen. He always maintained that he inherited a large part of his make-up from her, so it is not surprising that he holds her in particularly affectionate remembrance. It is clear from her letters that she was most anxious that her son should inherit her own lively cultural and artistic interests and her unusually strong links with other European countries. She was fluent in English and French, had travelled widely and had many English friends.

When he began to learn Latin she set to work to learn it with him. She enjoyed 'the logical structure of the language', but she added humorously, 'I hope that not all young girls and their lovers in ancient Rome had to speak like that'. His mother's last great joy was Reinold's letters from Paris, where he was a student at the Sorbonne in 1909. He told her about the lectures and about his daily visits to the Louvre. 'It is a great joy to me', she wrote to a friend, 'to see how the boy is developing with my own intense intellectual interests.'

The Trieglaff home into which Reinold's parents moved in 1906 was no longer the simple two-storied manor house of their grandfather's time, with the small veranda-like front. On to the old and somewhat modest house had been built a modern residence with tall windows, a pillared portico surmounted by an ornamental balcony, broad gables above a high staircase window, and an octagonal tower with a helmet-shaped dome and flagpole. In front there was a wide terrace ornamented with stone vases and overlooking a wide lawn with shady trees and sloping gently down to the lake. Near by were spacious farm buildings, labourers' cottages and the village with its two churches. All this formed a self-contained little world of its own. The nearest village and estate were several miles away across the fields of corn, turnips and potatoes, beyond the willows, woods and lines of trees. It was a broad land, not flat and unbroken, but dotted with lakes and streams, a country of short hot summers and long hard winters, with a wide, open landscape.

At Greifenberg, where his parents lived in the early years, Reinold made friends with Richard Schläfke, the son of a prison warder, with whose family he was boarded for two years. Greifenberg was a small town with about seven thousand inhabitants. It was a market town, the centre of the trade of an agricultural area. Reinold's mother boarded him with the Schläfke family with a definite object. 'If you want to achieve anything in life,' she said, 'you have got to know how ordinary people feel and think.'

To supplement the meagre salary of her husband, Frau Schläfke had to find additional sources of income; so she acted as cook for the prisoners. In summer she generally made cabbage soup for the 'boarders' in the cells, and she also took in lodgers. The warder's house was very small, so Reinold and his friend Richard were very glad when the prison was not very full. Then each of them could have a cell as living-room and bedroom. In later years, when Thadden made the acquaintance of the Gestapo, he liked to recall his former life in prison. 'I already had experience of living in a cell,' he said. 'There was nothing very surprising about it.'

After this stay at Greifenberg, Reinold went on to the Military Academy (*Ritterakademie*) at Brandenburg on the Havel, a boarding school founded in 1705 by King Frederick I of Prussia for the sons of Prussian nobility. The principle of exclusively limiting admission to the sons of the nobility had been modified in the middle of the nineteenth century, but nevertheless it was still mainly boys from the best families that thronged the cloisters of the old monastery beside the Havel, and sat on the hard benches of a school that for a good half-century had ranked with the best grammar schools of Prussia. The Military Academy was a school of Prussian rigour and severity. The schoolrooms and dormitories were drab and tasteless like barrack-rooms. Discipline was strict. The boys were wakened

Reinold von Thadden-Trieglaff

The Kirchentag assembly in Munich, 1959

at half past six in summer and winter alike, and 'lights out', even for the seniors, was at nine o'clock. Reinold was by no means a model pupil; he was much too easy-going, and he only shone in one subject—history.

Thadden only passed his *Abitur* (school-leaving examination) in 1909 by cribbing part of the outline for his literature essay from a friend. However, he returned to Pomerania; and the choice of a career did not cause him any anxiety. It was more or less obvious that he would study Law for a time as his father and many others of his class had done, and then get a commission in the army, preferably in an old cavalry regiment. Eventually, as a reserve officer, he could take over his father's estate. His future seemed clearly defined.

It was at Greifswald that Thadden first came into contact with the German Student Christian Movement. There was no accident in this. 'The winter session of 1911–12 was for me a time of self-examination,' he said later. 'Here in Pomerania the bearer of the name "Thadden" and the heir to the pietist tradition of Trieglaff must inevitably find himself involved with the most varied groups of people and influences. He declined an invitation from a Baron von Tiele-Winckler-Rothenmoor to attend a pietist mission on his estate in Mecklenburg.[1] 'There was nothing in it for me,' he said. Then a medical student, a former Guards officer, a man of rigid and rather narrow views, attached himself to Reinold. 'Whenever he saw me enjoying a glass of beer with a few friends, he would walk past with his brow wrinkled in disapproval, as if to say "They have not been really 'awakened'."' Thadden found this pietism had little connection with the great questions of the day and he called it an 'almost private Christianity'.

These attempts to draw him this way or that had their counterpart in the difficulties and uncertainties with which he was struggling in his own heart. He would walk for hours along the old city walls seeking an answer to the question 'Where do I belong?'

[1] The Tiele-Winckler family were in touch with revivalist movements in England and Wales in the 1890s.

Faith did not come to him simply and naturally as part of his pietist inheritance. He speaks of hours of bitterness 'when heaven seemed silent'. In one such period of depression an old friend of the family, George Michaelis, advised him to try the German Student Christian Movement.

George Michaelis, who was Imperial Chancellor in 1917, had been a close friend of Reinold's father since they were junior lawyers together in Frankfurt. Adolf von Thadden seems to have rather looked up to his friend as the stronger personality. Anyway, he usually took his friend's advice, which was offered often enough. Every autumn Michaelis came to Trieglaff for partridge shooting and Bible study; and whenever the Thaddens went to Berlin they visited the Michaelis home there.

George Michaelis was an example of the best type of Prussian government official. He could remember exactly when he was converted. It was at Liegnitz that he 'came to a clear recognition of the will of God and a joyful acceptance of it for himself', and he did not hesitate a moment to work out in his daily life the full implications of his change of heart. When he gave up smoking and drinking vintage wine his friends and neighbours could well put this down to personal idiosyncrasy, but when he gave up the chairmanship of the *Ressource*, a popular social club, and told the President flatly that he would no longer attend the stag-parties, dinners and state balls, it seemed to the self-satisfied society of 1914 little short of a public insult. In his memoirs Michaelis maintains that 'a genuine conversion requires greater courage than that traditional affair of honour, a pistol duel'. Thadden had in a sense inherited his father's friendship with Michaelis; indeed, he felt closer perhaps to 'Uncle George', as he called him, than to his father. During Thadden's last year at Greifswald Michaelis became Chairman of the German Student Christian Movement in succession to Count Pückler; so when his old friend's son told him about his religious difficulties he very naturally suggested that the SCM might be helpful.

The German SCM, as Thadden came to know it at Greifswald, was not yet predominantly a theological students' club. It contained students from the faculties of Languages, Law and Medicine. He found there also his second cousin Gottfried Handtmann, a theological student, of whom Thadden said that membership of the SCM meant for him as a divinity student much less of a 'confession' than it would be for a member of another faculty. They used to meet in a little room in the Nikolai-church, just a few of them, each with his Bible, and among them was law student Reinold von Thadden.

Although Thadden was later to be Michaelis' successor as Chairman of the SCM, his connection with the movement was at first somewhat loose. He was in his last year and his final examination was approaching. At the time the examiner seemed more important than the 'brother with the Bible'. Yet the SCM provided the background for an incident in which for the first time he came up against firmly established convention on his own responsibility and by his own decision. This was the affair of the duel.

At noon on October 11th, 1912, Adolf von Thadden came home to Trieglaff with terrible news. Reinold and his old friend and fellow student Jürgen von Blanckenburg had been challenged to a sabre duel by a corps student named von Langermann. Blanckenburg had accepted the challenge immediately, but Reinold had declined on grounds of conscience. The scandal in the university and throughout the whole patrician and academic world was unimaginable. A Thadden refusing a duel! A promising lawyer running away! A nobleman who would not fight! In the Kaiser's Germany this was absolutely impossible. It was as good as social suicide. In a letter Reinold's grandmother Marie wrote: 'You can imagine what the consequences will be for our Reinold. A thorny path in the army, no chance to become a reserve officer, difficulty in getting a government appointment—and in future he will be defenceless against the "rowdies", who will be able to strike him across the face with their riding-whips with impunity! That is the worldly side; but think also of the other, a clear conscience, fellowship with the living God, solidarity with Christian friends, and worth-while tasks to fulfil in the Kingdom of God.'

The whole affair had one good result. It brought Reinold and his father more closely together than they had been for a long time. Reinold's father completely understood his son's attitude; but he also realized its inevitable consequences, though he pulled every possible string on his behalf. They went together to Berlin and called on a whole series of influential people.

Looking back on this incident in later years, Thadden thus assessed the influence it exerted on his life. 'The refusal of the duel and all the fuss it caused was of little actual importance. It had little effect on me. What was important for me was the profession of faith that underlay it. Sooner or later a genuine confession had to be opposed to the caricature of honour that this challenge represented.'

Meanwhile, after the first excitement had died down, he took his final examination and started work as a junior lawyer in the Greifenberg court. Then he became a soldier.

Thadden's first period of military service was a single-handed struggle against the spectre of discredit that pursued him since his refusal of the duel at Greifswald. It was a fight against prejudice and convention, a dispute between an individual with the courage of his convictions and the fossilized conception of honour current at the time. He was in fact taking a lone stand against the code of honour of the Prussian officer clique, into which it was assumed that a son of the house of Thadden should be accepted. That he eventually achieved this object was due partly to the indefatigable efforts of his father, and even more to the sympathetic intervention of the Kaiser, William II.

Thadden wanted to serve in a regiment in which he had the prospect of eventually becoming a reserve officer. His father applied first to the Bromberg Mounted Grenadiers, only to meet with a blank refusal. His second application to the 12th Dragoons at Gnesen looked more promising. The commanding officer, Colonel von Maltzahn, told him: 'Your son will encounter no unpleasantness here, and anyone with the right gifts can become a reserve officer.'

The Colonel had evidently not understood the case at all. That was obvious soon after Thadden's arrival at Gnesen as a one-year volunteer in the autumn of 1913. Almost all the other one-year men were corps students; and they soon realized who he was, for the story of the refusal of the duel had been spread round the student corps in all the universities. Thadden found himself isolated. In the officers' mess he sat silent. On duty he received only the minimum essential communications, and off duty most of his comrades avoided him like the plague. The tension eventually snapped one evening in the officers' club, when one of his chief tormentors threw a glass of champagne in his face. Thadden went back to the barracks, but his young comrades followed him and wrecked his room. Thadden reported the incident through 'official channels' and the adjutant gave the one-year men a mild reprimand. Things did improve a little, but Thadden was very glad when the initial training was over and he was able to exercise the treasured privilege of one-year volunteers and rent a room in the town. By that means he reduced the contacts with the other cadets to a minimum, and curtailed considerably the opportunities for unpleasantness. A little later they went over to field exercises, which meant a good deal of riding in the open air instead of being cooped up together indoors.

On the whole Thadden enjoyed his army service. He was in a cavalry regiment stationed near the frontier; and soon, in the summer of 1914, the Russian invasion of East Prussia provided first-class training for the future officers. Thadden's regiment was sent to the battle front, not after all to the East, but to Flanders and northern France. They took part in the advance into Belgium in support of the 4th Infantry Division. This was Thadden's first introduction to the country in which he was to have such poignant and for him significant experiences in the Second World War. On a patrol through Malines in August 1914 his horse was shot under him. He fell and was seriously wounded, bleeding profusely; but he managed to elude the pursuing Belgians. For a time he had to go into hospital in Brussels; but he recovered in time to take part in the Battle of the Marne and the retreat of von Kluck's army.

If he had had the idea that his personal situation might improve on active service, he was soon disillusioned. He did indeed become an NCO; but when the other one-year volunteers of the same age were made acting sergeants, he was the only one left out.

A little later, when the regiment was at Noyon, the acting sergeants of Thadden's year were promoted to second lieutenants. On the same day, Thadden, who was still an NCO, was ordered to take two men and clean out the latrines. As he was standing in the trench a distant cousin of his, Captain Count Hahn-Schwirsen, rode past. 'What are you doing here?' he asked. 'I thought you were all officers now.' 'Not I,' answered Thadden. 'Then I don't know what's the matter with you all!' he said, and rode on.

Now Reinold's father took a hand. He sent a petition to the Kaiser with the signatures of influential friends. Then he packed his uniform and drove to Berlin, and with the help of Michaelis and other friends he obtained an invitation to General Headquarters. He did not see the Kaiser personally; but he was able to explain his son's difficulties to the Chancellor, Bethmann-Hollweg, and von Valentini, the chief of the Civil Cabinet, and also Grand Admiral von Tirpitz and a number of other influential officers and diplomats who were in close touch with the Kaiser. He gave each of them a copy of his petition, and a list of friends who were willing to testify to his son's blameless character and his suitability for a commission.

Adolf von Thadden was quite at home at General Headquarters. Nearly all the officers and officials in the Kaiser's entourage were friends, relatives or acquaintances, representatives of old Prussian noble families. He was welcomed everywhere and a chair was set for him in the mess with the High Command. He was even put into a staff car and driven over to Lille, where the 12th Dragoons were, to see his son. Everything seemed to be going so well that he wrote home triumphantly, 'Reinold will soon get his promotion.'

Meanwhile Reinold had further interviews with his commanding officer. The German divisions had been trying hard to force a break-through to Warsaw, and the regiment of Dragoons was now in reserve in the East. Once more the conversation turned on the single question that had become crucial for Thadden's military career.

Colonel: 'You want to become a reserve officer. That is only possible on one condition. You must withdraw your refusal of the duel at Greifswald and undertake to submit in future unconditionally to the Code of Honour of the Army. Can you give me this assurance?'

Thadden: 'Sir, I can neither revoke my refusal nor give you the assurance you require.'

Colonel: 'I will give you a minute to reflect. Will you not after all give me the assurance I ask for?'

Thadden: 'Sir, I have nothing more to say.'

Thadden was dismissed and rode thoughtfully through the night back to his squadron. It was Christmas Eve, 1914. Some days later, during an alert, the ensign from a neighbouring squadron, von Werder, hitherto one of Thadden's bitterest opponents, came riding up to him and said: 'I have held you in contempt up till now, because I thought you had refused the duel at Greifswald out of cowardice. I have heard how you behaved before the commanding officer and I realize that your decision was really a matter of conscience. I want to ask your forgiveness.'

It became known later that Thadden's second interview with his commanding officer arose out of an inquiry from the Military Cabinet. The 'Thadden Case' had actually been laid before the Kaiser, which was a unique occurrence. Ordinarily a sergeant was not regarded as a matter of immediate concern to the highest War-Lords.

A few months later Reinold von Thadden was promoted to Lieutenant in the 17th Dragoons.

Now at last the shadow of the duel affair was lifted from Thadden's life. He has always regarded this experience as having an important bearing on his whole life. He was not thinking so much of the social system of the day which showed itself in the confusing interplay of convention and patronage. It was distressing, of course, that a young man belonging to the favoured and privileged class should be placed at the mercy of the mysterious and unpredictable power of tradition, and should only have survived by the favour of relations and influential connections. What he himself found so significant, and what he regarded as an inestimable gain for his whole life was that he had proved his own strength of character by his steadfast refusal to clear away his difficulties by any formal compromise. However effective his father's far-reaching connections doubtless were, this witness to the loyalty to his convictions cannot have been without influence. In Thadden's life the duel episode and its consequences were the prologue to another test of his faith in the Church struggle against the Nazis twenty years later.

Thadden remained in the 17th Dragoons until the end of the war, taking part in the fighting in the Masuren marshes, the liberation of Memel, the battles of the Niemen salient north of Kowno, the cavalry fighting east of the Dubissa, the battle of Wilna, the attack on the Duna positions and the capture of Riga. It was a famous, if old-fashioned, regiment. Its Colonel-in-Chief was the Grand Duke of Mecklenburg, its commanding officer was Colonel von Heydebreck, the owner of vast estates, who had returned to active service at the outbreak of war, and the leader of the cavalry squadrons was Count Conrad Brockdorff-Ahlefeldt. Among the younger officers Thadden was particularly friendly with Count Alfred Waldersee. He seems to have found a sort of military home in the 4th squadron of the regiment. He says, 'I learned there a kind of manly comradeship. We were like a family.' His new comrades knew, of course, that there had been some sort of 'nasty business' associated with him, but Count Waldersee made the comment, 'We are only interested in the kind of man he is.' Count Waldersee was then a seventeen-year-old volunteer and he said of Thadden: 'Without our realizing it, within a fortnight he became our spiritual leader. We roughed it together, and we prayed together, which is something I had not done for years. We found him a friend and teacher, who took us by the hand and led us.'

During the second half of the war Thadden was with his regiment in the Baltic states. There was no military activity of any importance, and the routine duties bored him. In a letter written in May 1917 he said: 'We spend the morning in an officers' riding exercise under the Major, followed by a lecture in the open air by Lieutenant von Bülow about the achievements of the regiment during the campaign in Baden in 1849—particularly relevant, don't you think? And all very exhausting and unpleasant!'

During these years in the Baltic states, the enforced leisure of an officer in the army of occupation left Thadden time to worry increasingly about his own religious position. This is distinctly evident in his letters to his seventeen-year-old sister Ehrengard ('Eta'), in which he is always bringing up the question of his religious faith. 'It is impossible to imagine one's own death, for how can life form any picture of its opposite; but the natural fear of death has always impelled the human mind to think about eternity, the whence and whither of life. Hence the many religions; but to this problem only one man has found the complete answer which millions of people throughout the centuries have been seeking, which defied death and gave them peace in their hearts, and that was Jesus. Do you understand this? This is the basis of my faith How I long to make it clear to you!'

Strange words to come from a young lieutenant to his sister! But they already show the missionary zeal which was characteristic of Thadden.

2

THE TENEMENTS OF BERLIN

AFTER six years in the army, Reinold von Thadden returned to his native Pomerania. It had changed considerably, but so had he. The régime which he had served had collapsed; the Kaiser, through whose personal intervention alone he had become an officer, had abdicated. The landowning aristocracy, personified by his father, had lost much of its influence. He was welcomed with red flags by the new rulers—the workers', soldiers' and peasants' councils.

It was no different in Pomerania from anywhere else in Germany; but in this predominantly agricultural area, still largely conditioned by the ownership of great estates, the slogans of the revolution were directed primarily at one serious grievance, the backward social conditions of the agricultural workers in many parts of the province.

Urged on by agitators from outside, this pent-up anger over the injustice of conditions on many estates and the lack of understanding on the part of so many landowners was directed against guilty and innocent alike.

At Trieglaff it is fair to say that a genuinely pleasant relationship between the Thadden family and their tenants had existed for many years and there was very little feeling of hostility towards the landlord; but other areas experienced many expressions of anger over the injustice of conditions on some of the great estates.

Thadden had already seen something of revolution in the Baltic states. There he had also met the man who as agent of the provisional government in Berlin was given the task of cleaning up the

German position in Pomerania. Herr August Winnig, a bricklayer who had gained a leading position in the trade unions and in the Social Democratic Party, had first achieved prominence as a publicist during the war. His aim was to make the German worker a conscious participant in the fateful struggle of his nation, or in his own words 'to bring the working class into the Reich'. In the Baltic states he met with considerable opposition from the officers and particularly from the staff of the cavalry brigade in which Thadden was an aide-de-camp.

Nevertheless, Thadden and his fellow officer Lorenz-Meyer decided to take a closer look at the 'red embassy' from Berlin, so they went to the first general meeting of the Baltic 'Soldiers' Council'. They had a great surprise. Of course, much of what Winnig said was the usual revolutionary propaganda; but then suddenly he began to attack the Bolsheviks, and drew a picture of the working-class problem that made a deep impression on the two young officers. Thadden wrote: 'It came suddenly clear to us how much had been neglected hitherto', and after that he became more and more convinced that if the revolution were to be overcome its lessons must be learned.

When he came home to Trieglaff he described himself as 'a passionate Conservative social revolutionary—a horrible description, but I could find no better'. He was still basically a Conservative; but coupled with that now was a firm resolve to take social questions seriously and to do something towards their solution.

He found at home a receptive soil for his ideas. In the last years of the war his sister Elizabeth, who had managed the Trieglaff home since her mother's death, had organized a movement with the help of grandmother Marie (now eighty-four years old) to bring town children into the country. As usually happens in such cases, the founders had to do most of the work at first, and 'Bring town children into the country' became 'Bring town children to Trieglaff'. Most of the children came from the working-class area of East Berlin.

In the autumn of 1919, Thadden went to Berlin to become

secretary of a youth training course organized by the Social Work Association. He found Berlin still shaken by the fever of revolution. Left-wing demonstrations, strikes and riots were of daily occurrence. There were signs of a complete collapse of the national currency, and the beginnings of the Kapp revolt, that disastrous adventure of right-wing hotheads, were already discernible on the horizon. No wonder Thadden was uneasy about going into East Berlin, the hot-bed of Communism. 'I hope my future landlord will only be a very moderate Bolshevik, and in the event of a revolution will stick to the milder principle of just murdering his guest in bed instead of roasting him first,' he wrote in a letter home.

In reality this twenty-eight-year-old son of a Pomeranian landowner came with a wide-open heart to the capital of his country, the centre of misery in a time of serious national distress. He did not want just to see and hear; he wanted to do his modest share in helping to reconstruct.

Siegmund-Schultze, the chief of the Social Work Association, brought young Thadden into his group of voluntary workers. He had set up a sort of private system of voluntary probation officers in connection with the juvenile courts, and after serving their sentence young offenders were allocated to one or other of these members of the Social Work Association. It was their task to help them to become good citizens again, and if possible to persuade them to join one of the youth clubs that had been opened in various districts of East Berlin. In addition Thadden's legal assistance was available to the juvenile courts in connection with the cases of young delinquents.

So it was that Thadden found himself going round the tenements and back-yards near the Warsaw Bridge—upstairs, downstairs, knocking now on this door now on that, talking to youngsters, questioning parents, relatives and lodging-house keepers. These were heart-breaking missions into haunts where want and vice, poverty and crime, misery and debt, lived side by side. Then in the evening he went to the youth clubs, reasoning with suspicious or unco-operative boys, holding Bible classes for his fellow workers and local residents, discussing routine duties and giving instruction to future youth leaders.

At first Thadden did not attempt to sort out the complex mass of vivid impressions to which he was subjected; 'otherwise I could not endure the mental and spiritual strain'. In addition Berlin was full of ferment and seething unrest, both political and spiritual. Everywhere there were clashes of opinion and creed. In large groups and small there was endless discussion and debate, constructive and destructive arguments, quarrels and disputes. Thadden was soon drawn into this whirlpool of factions, parties and programmes. Indeed, it seems as if in his eagerness to hear and learn he deliberately threw himself into this vortex of debating clubs. One evening he went to a meeting of the right-wing Free Germans. The next, he listened for five hours to a discussion between Socialists and members of the People's Party on 'Privilege versus Communism'. He turned up at a debate organized by the League of Peace on 'Pan-Germanism and pacifist ethics'. Then again he got himself involved in a discussion with some English Quakers about the League of Nations, a subject of particular interest to him in view of a thesis he was preparing for a doctor's degree.

In the summer of 1914 Lance-Corporal von Thadden had been a guest at the wedding of his friend Kameke in Thüngen, a village in the sunny valley of the Wern, near the country seat of the Franconian Baron von Thüngen. In August 1920 he was there again, officially for treatment at the spa at Brückenau for blood poisoning contracted on the estate of his aunt Oertzen. Actually he was looking for a wife. He wrote to his youngest sister: 'You can understand why I want to settle down and have a firm foundation for my life.'

Even in this matter he was not one to follow his feelings blindly. He had very firm and decided views on marriage. He observed: 'Differences of class and origin, disagreements with relations-in-law and difficult circumstances can all be overcome without wrecking a marriage; but one thing is essential for a life-long sharing of difficulties and responsibilities, for the growth of mutual confidence and for the attainment of eternal happiness. That is similarity of temperament, not necessarily of intelligence or interests, but harmony at the centre of one's being, a longing for communion with God, for truth, purity and strength.' He would not have been the honest critic that he was if he had not applied this test to himself. 'My greatest difficulty in choosing the right partner is in myself. I am a Conservative but also a believer in social progress. I am an aristocrat and at the same time I have conscientious obligation to the people. I am a Christian and yet feel freely responsible to God alone. I am a traditionalist with an open mind on all kinds of questions of science and philosophy. Consequently I might marry almost any type of girl with a reasonable chance of happiness or unhappiness according to which side of my nature was uppermost when I made my choice!'

And so, while at Brückenau in 1920, he paid an early visit to Heilsberg, the little white castle overlooking the valley of the Sinn, where Elizabeth von Thüngen lived, the daughter of Baron Rudolf von Thüngen. He had met her at the wedding of his friend Kameke in 1914. He now found himself in an actively Christian home. Elizabeth's father was formerly a Bavarian colonel and Court Chamberlain. The University of Erlangen had conferred an honorary Doctorate on him in recognition of his research into the history of Franconia. For some years he had attended the General Synod at Ansbach as delegate from his local Lutheran church. At Heilsberg, however, the dominant personality was Elizabeth's mother, formerly Princess zu Ysenburg-Büdingen and closely related to a number of noble families including the ruling houses of Lippe and Schleswig-Holstein. She owed her very individual form of Christian faith to her earlier contacts with leading figures of the pietist movement about the turn of the century.

A few days at Heilsberg in August 1920 were enough for Reinold to become enchanted with Elizabeth von Thüngen. 'I have found what I was looking for,' he wrote happily to his sister Eta. 'We love each other.' The engagement was celebrated at Heilsberg, and soon after she was introduced to Reinold's friends and relations in Pomerania.

It was the beginning of a marriage of great happiness. The first children arrived during comparatively tranquil years. But Thadden was soon involved in the troubles around the coming to power of Adolf Hitler. He could scarcely help being involved, for this Pomeranian aristocrat was also a leader of German student life, as we shall now see.

3

THE STUDENTS' FATHER

THADDEN's association with the leadership of the German Student Christian Movement began in the spring of 1923 with a letter from George Michaelis, who had been living in Saarow in Brandenburg since his retirement from the position of lord lieutenant of Pomerania. The letter announced the engagement of his daughter Lotte to Hermann Weber, who was a minister and the general secretary of the German SCM. Thadden went to Berlin to convey the congratulations of the family, and met Weber there. 'We took to each other at once', he says. Hermann Weber became Thadden's life-long friend. 'He was my other self.' The two men were of almost the same age, but of quite different social position and origin—one the owner of a great estate, the other a parson; one descended from a line of noble ancestors, the other the son of a south German merchant vintner.

Very soon their friendship was deepened through their association in a common task, for when Weber said 'We need younger men in the SCM. Will you help?' Thadden at once agreed. What neither his brief contact with the SCM at Greifswald nor the efforts of the Chairman Michaelis had been able to do, this friendship with the minister from Baden brought about. Thadden became an enthusiast for the SCM. In August of the same year he and Weber presented a report to the SCM conference at Schneverdingen on 'guilt and fate as factors in the present distress'. The following January he was elected to the executive committee; and a year later he became one of the vice-presidents in association with Paul Humburg, a former

Von Thadden
as Commandant
of Louvain

Conference on *Jews and Christians* at the Berlin Kirchentag, 1961

A Press Conference at the Berlin Kirchentag, 1961
(Left to right: von Thadden, the author as chairman of the publicity committee, Dr Kurt Scharf the chairman of the council of the Protestant Churches in Germany, Dr Hans Hermann Walz the general secretary of the Kirchentag.)

The Essen Kirchentag, 1950

general secretary of the SCM and afterwards Presiding Bishop of the Rhineland Church.

The German SCM was the spiritual child of the German Evangelical revival in the nineteenth century. It was founded and led by pietists. It was now a branch of the World's Student Christian Federation, dedicated to definite missionary work in the universities and colleges, but independent of any official church. It was a minority group with never more than between 1,500 and 2,000 members, and had been strongly influenced by its first two chairmen, Count Eduard von Pückler and George Michaelis. Both of these men, as Thadden said, adopted a 'paternal attitude to the students, which was combined both with great spiritual authority and superior and highly respected social positions'.

When Thadden began work with the German SCM, it was still mainly supported by the war-time generation. In the summer session of 1922 35 per cent of the older members were ex-service men. Classified by faculties in the largest group, 37.5 per cent were theological students, the technical faculties provided 33.5 per cent, the arts faculties 20 per cent, the faculties of law 6.5 per cent, medicine 6 per cent and agriculture 5 per cent.

At this time the German SCM was strongly affected by the intense intellectual conflicts of the post-war period and particularly the current trend towards socialism. One secretary of the time, Johannes Kühne, recalls a lecture given at the first SCM conference in 1919 at Bad Oeynhausen by Eberhard Arnold, a member of the SCM committee, on 'A Socialist interpretation of the Sermon on the Mount'. This Arnold, whom Thadden replaced on the committee in 1924, had the Christian Student Magazine *The Furrow* published with a flaming red cover in 1918.

In the international field the German SCM had to define its attitude to the general mistrust of Germany and the Germans and the unhappy psychological consequences of the Treaty of Versailles. At the first post-war conference of the European SCMs in Holland in 1921 the small German delegation made a vain attempt to elicit an unbiased statement about the differing views about war guilt. They had to content themselves with a declaration that the leaders of the Student Christian Movement in America and England had condemned the Treaty of Versailles as unjust. At the first post-war meeting of the Central Committee of the World's Student Christian Federation in Peking in 1922, Michaelis, who led the German delegation, had to threaten that he would withdraw from the conference if no declaration was made against the 'lying spirit' of Versailles. But the representatives of seven nations, including America, England and France, declared their disbelief in the sole responsibility of Germany for the war.

'Was not the hidden bond of our Berlin SCM group in 1923, and also its strength and its comparative limitations, the fact that we were a community of ex-service men, who had been through the 1914–18 war as committed Christians?' This was the question Thadden put to Weber a few years later, as they recalled and sought to explain the unforgettable steadfastness of the SCM. At the time this background of a terrific common experience affected even the language in which they both spoke to the students. Hermann Weber had been an officer on the Western Front all through the war, and he used to refer to his office work in Berlin with a soldier's contempt as 'the paper work of the General Staff round the green table'. Whenever he could he went into the 'front line', i.e. to conduct Bible classes and pastoral discussions in the universities. Thadden's speeches and writings are full of expressions borrowed from army life. 'We have our own orders to attack.' 'We are responsible for that particular section of the battle-front to which we have been posted by our eternal Commander.' 'We are waging a war of allies on the battlefield of the academic world, with a variety of auxiliary armies.'

Another point on which Thadden and Weber were in complete harmony was what Thadden called 'the question of the laity'. They shared a 'passionate desire to make the man in the pew and even outside the church doors share responsibility for "his" church'. To Thadden as a lawyer and farmer this seemed a matter of course, but it was not less so to the Baden pastor. 'It must be the aim of the Church,' he said, 'to fulfil her allotted task in all professions and classes, parties and factions, and this can only be done through people who give faithful service in their own immediate situation. "Missionaries" sent into the academic world or to the masses cannot do this alone. What is needed is men who are completely involved in the situation and who feel an inescapable compulsion to accept the responsibility of bearing witness in that situation. To call men to this service and to sustain them in it is the most important task of the Church.'

There were two items of special importance in the German SCM programme at that time. The first was the courses for group leaders at the universities, which provided theological preparation for the work of the session. The other was the big annual Summer Conferences, which were the real high spot of the work of the SCM, and which were attended by hundreds of students from all the German universities. One of the first members of the SCM, Theophil Mann, said with good reason that anyone who set out to write the history of the SCM would have to begin with the sentence, 'In the beginning was the conference'.

Thadden took the fullest part in all these activities from the first. Dr Hanns Lilje, now Bishop of Hanover, has written: 'The astonishing thing was that Thadden was quite at home in any students' forum, which is perhaps the most difficult to be found anywhere. He might well be called upon to hold a Bible class in the SCM group or give a public lecture at one of the universities. Nobody seemed to ask whether he could do it. That was assumed as a matter of course. *He had the peculiar quality, which is so very important in dealing with students, the quality of self-criticism.*'

Thadden's election as Chairman produced surprisingly little by way of drastic change. Although he had complained so anxiously about the lack of leadership in the SCM, he proved anything but a hard and exacting Chairman. 'He was very efficient but unobtrusive.' 'He always made decisions, but without any fuss.' 'His real leadership showed itself in a combination of humility and decision.' These are the opinions of men who worked with him at the time.

Meanwhile Thadden saw with clear and absolute honesty the defects and faults of the German SCM. He complained of the 'musty spirit' in many branches. In a letter to Weber he wrote half angrily and half sadly that the 'accumulated lumber' must be swept away. He spoke scornfully of the 'proud participation of some ten old comrades' in an 'Old Comrades' Conference' at Köslin. 'What is the value of our whole Old Comrades organization if they just stagnate in edifying ideologies without doing anything to help lonely and worried brethren?'

Thadden's next colleague in the SCM was Hanns Lilje, then a young pastor from Hanover and chaplain to the Technical High School there. Michaelis had brought him to Berlin in 1927 to be Weber's successor. Looking back over this period, the present Bishop of Hanover has said: 'My meeting with Thadden was one of the most important events in my life.' The centre of Thadden's activity in the SCM was his capacity to gain people's confidence. He was re-elected Chairman year after year, which was by no means as much to be taken for granted as it appears today. He had the ability to handle all sorts of people with ease, whether they were important public figures or leaders of the Church.

Thadden's diary during these years, if such existed, would show an astonishing pattern of engagements. He was always travelling, not in order to build up big new organizations, but usually to help small and scattered groups or even individuals. His work was unobtrusive and almost unnoticed. For example, he visited groups of Old Comrades in Schleswig-Holstein. He held meetings for Bible study for students at his old university of Greifswald. He lectured on 'A Christian view of the race problem' to an academic conference at Bad Doberan in Mecklenburg. He gave three lectures at a provincial conference at Leba in Pomerania. He visited SCM branches at Mannheim, Karlsruhe, Darmstadt, Freiburg and Marburg. At another SCM conference in Leipzig he gave a lecture on 'Christianity and Politics'. He addressed SCM branches and groups of Old Comrades at Danzig, Elbing and Königsberg. He gave public lectures everywhere, but 'the work that gave me most satisfaction was the Bible study classes and private personal conversations. The way in which students quickly gained confidence and then brought out their most intimate and vital problems was most moving. I think that the "cure of souls" is not too extravagant a name for this work and I have an inner conviction that I have at least as much qualification for it as anyone else. It is a pity that I have not more opportunities for it, but who knows what life may have in store. Anything is possible these days.'

The more he travelled for the SCM and the more often he appeared at the universities and at conferences, the more he was sought after by other religious bodies. 'I am gradually being called to every second conference,' he said in 1927.

This was at the same time as he was struggling to save his estates, and trying to solve the problem of the inheritance. He was also elected a member of the Synod of the Pomeranian Church and in addition took his share in local politics.

It would be a mistake to imagine Thadden, the 'students' father', as they called him, as doing nothing but teaching and preaching. He liked to be gay among the light-hearted students. Sometimes he would laugh aloud in the middle of the night at the recollection of some joke that one of the students had told during the evening. During the first air-raid exercises at Saarow in 1936 he was responsible for a humorous parody on the sentimental lines

In this world of darkness
We must shine
You in your small corner
And I in mine.

He had a leather suitcase 'from my own cows', an enormous Trieglaff heirloom weighing about a hundredweight, which he used to laugh about even more than the poor students who lugged it about out of respect for their chairman. At the beginning of 1933 he came to Edinburgh in company with a student, Georg Krause, now a minister in Meerane in Saxony. Thadden, who was a good sailor, gives an amusing description of the crossing. He shared a cabin with Krause and as they were leaving the Elbe estuary a storm blew up, making the poor student most unhappy. Thadden says, 'I woke in the morning feeling very cheerful and was just about to hold morning prayers, when I caught sight of a miserable-looking figure in the lower berth, his face a beautiful green colour. I thought to myself, the poor fellow is quite exhausted. I must get him something to eat, so I fetched from my suitcase a piece of smoked goose, that I had brought with me to eat on the journey, and held it up in front of Georg Krause's nose. The result was beyond description. For my part I enjoyed an excellent breakfast without any competition.'

When Thadden and Lilje were visiting Geneva they were invited to an official reception. For this Lilje wore a dinner jacket for the first time. Their comment was: 'To be suitably dressed produces a greater peace of mind than any religion in the world.'

The time soon came when the German SCM was to find itself between the political millstones. Its difficulties did not begin with the 30th of January 1933, when Hitler came to power. They began long before the swastika flags were hoisted on the German churches, and before Thadden was compelled to dissolve the membership of the SCM in the summer of 1938.

In his visits to SCM groups in the colleges and universities Thadden had come up against political questions ever since the end of the '20s, and whether he felt it to be consistent with the aims of the SCM or not, he could not avoid dealing with them. Among the topics of his lectures we have already noted such titles as *A Christian view of the race problem.* After 1933 there was hardly a meeting in which problems of the current political situation were not brought up.

The first real clash between the SCM and National Socialism occurred in June 1933 at the Summer Conference at Hammelburg in Bavaria. The conflict between Nazis and the Church had not yet flared up, but already considerable misgiving and anxiety was evident in many religious circles. Only a few days later Dr Fritz von Bodelschwingh would be forced to retire from the position of Reichsbishop after scarcely a month in office, in order to make way for the 'trusted follower of the Führer', Ludwig Müller, a chaplain from Königsberg. A few weeks later, in the scandalously rigged church elections of 23rd July, 1933, the attempt would be made to allocate all the key positions in the Protestant Church to Nazi 'German Christians', and only a few months later Martin Niemöller, the minister from Berlin-Dahlem, was to give the signal for resistance by an appeal for the formation of a Ministers' Defence League.

Thus it was just before the storm that the five hundred Christian students from all the German colleges and universities assembled at Hammelburg—to be met with one surprise after another. The camp, which had been made available by the YMCA, turned out to be closely integrated into the National Socialist movement and was in charge of SS and SA men in uniform. None of the important advertised speakers turned up. On the second day, when Lilje was leading a discussion on the election of the Reichsbishop, the tension became so serious that he had to abandon the idea of asking the students for a vote of confidence in Bodelschwingh.

It was in other ways an unusual conference. There were torch-light processions and telegrams of loyalty both to Hitler and Bodelschwingh. It was also the occasion of a stern rejection of the new dictator. W. A. Visser 't Hooft, the minister of the Dutch Reformed Church, who was secretary of the World's Student Christian Federation (and is now general secretary of the World Council of Churches), had come to Hammelburg directly after a meeting with Himmler in Munich. In front of a crowd of students preparing for a torchlight procession he asked Thadden what he thought of Hitler. Unhesitatingly and loudly, Thadden answered: 'He is the greatest charlatan in all history.' When Visser 't Hooft tried to hush him into greater caution, he repeated, still more loudly and clearly: 'The greatest charlatan in all history.'

No wonder that Thadden was glad when the conference was over. It had raised quite openly the question whether the work of the SCM was any longer possible in the universities and colleges of Nazi Germany. Compared with this fundamental question, the external details of its absorption into Nazi organizations were relatively unimportant, though the German SCM now faced the prospect of being drawn into the orbit of the 'National Socialist Student Unions', and Thadden had to face the prospect of being transformed from a simple Chairman into a Reich Commissar. He did actually attend a reception which Hitler arranged for the leaders of the Former Students' Associations. It was his one and only meeting with the dictator, and he came back horrified. He found Hitler's 'empty face' abhorrent.

What followed was to be expected. At the SCM council meeting on 20th–22nd July, 1933, in Berlin, Thadden faced a strong representation from Tübingen led by Professor D. Fezer, which demanded a change in the leadership of the SCM. The struggle continued for two days, then Thadden suspended himself 'from the exercise of all rights and functions of Chairman of the SCM' and gave all the secretaries leave of absence indefinitely. Fezer took over the leadership of the SCM. His task was to facilitate the incorporation of the SCM branches in the universities and colleges into the existing students' organizations in association with the Nazi German Student Organization.

In a brief report to his friend Weber in Freiburg, under the emotional impact of these events, Thadden wrote: 'The old SCM is finished for the present, because its whole basis has ceased to exist.'

Weber immediately raised objections. He thought Thadden had acted too precipitately. So did Rendtorff, Thadden's associate chairman. Thadden defended his action in a second and more detailed report. 'I went to Berlin following a telephone call, without knowing at all what was afoot. This only became clear in my discussions with Fezer. Nevertheless I believe that in the end my decision was based on a number of important objective reasons and neither on ignorance nor panic. I suppose the most important factor was my considered opinion that missionary work among the students would be futile without the possibility of reaching the individual within the student body through Bible study and preaching, by the formation of special groups and other forms of organization. I pictured to myself the new term in the autumn with a complete hamstringing of all SCM life throughout all the universities and colleges, if we failed to achieve a basis on which vigorous life is possible. It is quite clear to me on what lines we should work. We should accept no conditions that are incompatible with the

Gospel and with the essential nature of the Church of Christ, and in my opinion it is the duty of the leaders of the SCM to safeguard that and the freedom of the movement. If the conditions of absorption into the new student organization are conscientiously intolerable to us, then the SCM has reached the breaking-point.'

This still sounds like the final slamming of the door by an angry man. Nevertheless some months later Thadden was on the way to Tübingen to make one more attempt to avert the doom of the SCM. He had two interviews with Fezer at the Adolf Schlatter Hostel, the headquarters of the Tübingen SCM, where already the SA was in complete charge. He appealed to Fezer, arguing that conditions in the SCM had become impossible and that everything was at a standstill. He demanded that Fezer should relinquish his office. Fezer hesitated. He accused Thadden of lack of understanding of the resurgence of youth. Thadden persisted. He said, 'I have two days free. Tomorrow I will see you again.' Next day Fezer gave way, although he did not accept Thadden's arguments. He said that, because the majority of the students were for the moment against the new programme, he would not stand in the way. Thadden went back to Berlin. He was Chairman of the SCM again.

What was happening at this time to the SCM was being experienced also by many thousands of clubs and organizations. The spiritual dilemma into which many of the leaders and members of the SCM were forced was more important than the changes made in leadership or organization. What that meant for individual SCM members, and how they were driven to adopt a curious double-faced attitude, has been described by Wilhelm Giesen, a medical student in Berlin. 'Ostensibly all the members of the SCM were in the SA, the Brownshirts, even though some had paraded only for a few days or even hours. In Berlin we formed a sort of Brownshirt group of our own for the "personal indoor protection" of the SCM. For instance we sat like a brown phalanx round Pastor Jacobi, the minister of the Kaiser William Memorial Church in Berlin, when he was attacked. The same thing happened when Niemöller was driven out of his church and forbidden to preach. We sat with him in the garden of the parsonage, drinking tea and plainly visible in our SA uniforms. We were discussing the question whether the murder of a tyrant could ever be reconciled with the teaching of the Bible. The tyrant we were thinking of was obviously Hitler. It was indeed a crazy dilemma in which we found ourselves, and it is still difficult to realize how it could all have happened.'

Thadden was inevitably drawn into this dilemma, to which there seemed to be no rational solution. Whenever he visited the SCM hostel at Saarow, he found the members regularly carrying out the new military routine. There was a programme of duties, with reveille and flag parades and salutes to the Führer. When Thadden arrived he was urged to conform to the new routine and he did so. One morning he turned out at the flag-hoisting parade dressed in the uniform of a leader of the Stormtroopers (SA). But next day he took the uniform home in his suitcase, and never put it on again. This one occasion when he put on SA uniform remained an isolated concession that can only be understood against the background of mad confusion of those days, in which, as Wilhelm Giesen said: 'The great thing was that we were able to hold together. That was only possible under Thadden's leadership. He gave us confidence and taught us to trust each other.'

Indeed, the German SCM was able to continue its work among students until the end of 1938.

Thadden considers that one of the most important results of his work with the German SCM was that he was able to make contact at first hand with the younger generation of leading World Churchmen. Of course, he had already met some of the older leaders of the ecumenical movement, thanks particularly to Siegmund-Schultze's connections with the English-speaking world. But it was the German SCM, which had been from the first a member of the World's Student Christian Federation, that really became for him the gateway to the world. It gave him the friendship of a circle of younger men and women in England, France and America who were to be the pioneers of unity in Christendom during the next few years.

The man who drew him into this field of activity was Hanns Lilje, who had visited England, America and India. Thadden often grumbled that Lilje spent much more time travelling about the world than he did in his office in Berlin; but all the same he always did his utmost to make Lilje's journeys possible. 'Who knows,' he said apprehensively, 'how often during the next few years shall we still be in a position to take an active part in the work of the Federation outside Europe?'

In this wider field, too, Thadden's ability to create an atmosphere of confidence was immediately effective. Lilje has recorded this impression of Thadden's influence at two conferences during these difficult times. One was the British SCM Conference at Edinburgh in 1933, where Lilje spoke on 'Christendom and Communism'. The other was the meeting of the WSCF central committee at La Châtaigneraie, in Switzerland, soon after the National Socialist *coup* in Germany. 'During these months,' Lilje wrote, 'when every German was eyed askance, Thadden appeared quite unembarrassed. This was particularly important at Edinburgh, when all eyes were turned in apprehension on the approaching revolution in Germany. Both here and at La Châtaigneraie Thadden went about quite cheerfully. Once he climbed up on to a ten-foot diving board, gave the Hitler salute, and plunged into the water. It was just a student's joke, and was received as such; and it cheered and brightened and relaxed the atmosphere. In such ways Thadden won Christian confidence in the face of what was happening in Germany. It is due largely to him that the bond between the German SCM and the other Student Christian Movements in the world remained unbroken during the dark years ahead.'

During the difficult years that followed Thadden met in Germany many of the leading foreign Christian personalities, among them Dr George Bell, Bishop of Chichester, Eivind Berggrav, Bishop of Oslo, Dr Erling Eidem, Archbishop of Uppsala, and John R. Mott, President of the YMCA. These meetings often took place in modest hotels or in discreet private houses. Only with Dr Mott, the Grand Old Man of world Christendom, was it safe to venture openly into the Kaiserhof Hotel in Berlin. Here on one occasion

Thadden casually began eating before all the others had taken their places. Lilje nudged his neighbour and said, 'That's the privilege of the old nobility. You wouldn't know that.'

When Thadden checks off the names of leading personalities in the ecumenical movement who like himself came into it from the SCM, he often says: 'We are all out of the same box.' Thadden himself puts at the top of the list Dr William Temple, Archbishop of York and Canterbury. Temple had impressed him profoundly ever since his first vital contact with the English-speaking world at the Edinburgh Conference in 1933.

Next comes Willem A. Visser 't Hooft, with whom Thadden worked so closely in Geneva in 1946–48; then Suzanne de Diétrich, daughter of an industrialist in Lorraine, who was the head of the French SCM and is today one of the foremost Bible expositors in Europe.

Two other names Thadden mentions specially: Pierre Maury and Robert C. Mackie. To Maury, the President of the Reformed Church in France until his death in 1956, Thadden feels that he owes a greater inspiration than almost any other man. During the Second World War, when he was Commandant of Louvain, he visited Maury in Paris many times, a risky thing for a German officer to do, since Maury was a bitter opponent of the Nazi régime. 'After all that has happened,' Thadden wrote after his first visit to Maury in 1942, 'it was a wonderful experience to discover that there was no fundamental division within the Church of God, as we had learned to understand it.'

Robert Mackie was also a friend from the Geneva days. He is the man who has done much to introduce into his native Scotland a 'Kirk Week' on the model of the German Kirchentag.

Among the wider contacts that Thadden made in these years was one of particular interest to him later. In 1956 there was trouble over the admission to the Kirchentag at Frankfurt of members of congregations in the East Zone of Germany. Thadden referred the matter to Herr Hegen, the Zone Secretary for Internal Affairs and, later, ambassador in Warsaw. During their conversation at Pankow, in East Berlin, Hegen suddenly asked his visitor whether he had ever been to Prague before 1933. Thadden said he had. 'And what were you doing in Prague?' Hegen inquired. 'As Vice Chairman of the World's Student Christian Federation, I gave an address to a number of Czech students.'

Hegen replied: 'I was among your audience then. As you can perhaps imagine, I was brought up a Roman Catholic. I went to Mass. At that time, in the early thirties, I found myself out of sympathy with the Catholic Church and decided to have a look at the Protestants. That is how I came to be in your meeting. You actually said at that time exactly what you are saying today. For that reason I believe you and am prepared to help you.'

4

UNDER THE NAZIS

IN September 1932 about twenty thousand people met in Stettin for the first Pomeranian provincial *Kirchentag*, or Church Rally. This was an enormous number compared with the traditional attendance at church assemblies, and only comparable with the mass parades that were being staged by both left- and right-wing parties in those troubled and feverish days. The principal speaker, sharing the platform with Superintendent D. Walter Kähler, was the Deputy President of the Pomeranian Provincial Synod, Reinold von Thadden-Trieglaff.

He had undertaken this task only after considerable hesitation. Apart from anything else, the enormous size of the audience worried him. He knew that many would be weighing his words critically. He was afraid that the National Socialists might try to use such a large assembly for propaganda purposes. His own intention was 'to proclaim clearly and definitely to all parties the message of the Gospel'. He took a great deal of trouble over his speech (as he always did with every public utterance). He wrote it out three times. And he did not mince his words.

'In view of the things that are happening around us, things that today pursue us as in a nightmare and tomorrow cast us powerless into the street, things that at one moment push us into the mass hysteria of the crowds and the next abandon us all the more pitilessly to the terrible solitude of death—in view of all these things, *has the Church anything to say*? Yes, this Church with which we have lost touch because we no longer understand its language, which has become so unreal with its old-fashioned customs and ceremonies, so out-of-date in its liturgies and symbolism from the sixteenth century, so irrelevant with its sermons and devotions, so tedious and aimless in its multiplicity of organizations and efforts.

'Have we not hated this Church of the eternal yesterday? Or, rather, have we not done the only possible thing left to an educated man to do, have we not shrugged our shoulders and pigeon-holed this historic museum piece from the long dead days of medieval darkness?

'And yet the Church remains. It is set right in the middle of our time, not high above the turmoil of the world, but right in the midst of the scientific development, the economic situation and the various forms of political organization amongst which we live.

'Everywhere, wherever we are living out our lives, wherever the farmer tills the soil, or the merchant competes for markets, wherever contracts are drawn up, or wills are contested, or income tax returns are filled in, wherever matrimonial difficulties are dealt with, or questions of birth and education, wherever the fates of nations are in the balance and we take our part weaving at the loom of history, there the Church has its message to deliver. *There and nowhere else lies the mission of the Church.*'

There is good reason for quoting Thadden's Stettin address before describing his activities in the struggle of the Church against National Socialism. It could well be claimed that this has been the theme of his whole life, a summary of his work as a Christian layman. At the same time it foreshadows his personal conduct in the approaching dispute with the Nazi State and its philosophy.

By 1933 Thadden had already served eight years in the synod of his Provincial Church. He had been elected in 1925 with a group known as 'The working party for a living People's Church'. At the same time he became a member of the provincial church council. The 'working party' had been started by Günther Holstein, an ecclesiastical and constitutional lawyer in Greifswald. Its aims were to revive the church councils, and to gain admission for the younger members of congregations to them.

In 1929 he was sent by the Pomeranian Synod to Berlin as delegate to the General Synod of the Church in Prussia. In his book

In a Hopeless Position? (Auf verlorenem Posten?) he gives a whimsical description of his first appearance in the great Prussian 'church parliament'. He tells how he, a landowner from Pomerania, only thirty-seven years old, 'was received into this assembly of septuagenarians as a surprising intrusion of hardly acceptable youthfulness'. He mentions his own great-uncle Joachim von Alvensleben, who received him with the comment 'Still too immature, my dear fellow!'

There is a good deal of humour in his description of the activities of the General Synod; but the reality was serious enough. It is clear from his letters to Weber what an 'enormously important experience' this synod was for him. He almost worked himself to death for it. At the same time there is evidence of a developing detachment from the synod, for which there was a profound reason. The man who tries so energetically to recall the layman to a sense of responsibility for the Church has nevertheless always held certain reservations with regard to the Church's addiction to 'parliamentary' procedure. What caused him disquiet at the time of the Berlin synod was the uncritical adoption of the forms of parliamentary procedure and the formation of rival groups distinguished, in his opinion, not by genuine doctrinal differences, but by considerations of ecclesiastical expediency and rivalry. In more recent synods what he has sometimes missed bitterly is a spirit of real brotherhood, without which there can be, he thinks, no synod, no genuine 'coming together' in the Church. Not that he wishes to minimize or deny genuine differences of opinion. In fact, he defends these, because they are necessary; but he cannot understand why differences of opinion, however real, have to lead to enmity in personal relationships. In his own words, 'What sort of a brotherhood is it, if one member of a synod refuses to shake hands with another, because he holds a different opinion? In this way there can be no synod.'

Not merely as an SCM chairman but also as a member of the synod, von Thadden inevitably found himself drawn into the Church conflict with Hitler. The Nazi attack on the Church was aimed first on Berlin. The destructive wave of 'conformity' (Gleichschaltung) and indoctrination spread more slowly over the rest of the country. The Nazis concentrated particularly on Prussia; at first the south of Germany was left surprisingly alone. In a letter to Hermann Weber Thadden found two reasons for this. 'Firstly, the enormous provincial church in Prussia offered a much more attractive area for attempts at political "conformity" than did the smaller Protestant churches in the south; and secondly it seemed wiser to avoid more rigorous coercion against the Church in the southern provinces, because much stronger resistance was to be expected in some areas where the influence of pietism was strong—even possibly amongst members of the National Socialist party—than was the case in the north.'

At the time when Thadden made this first diagnosis of the Church's coming struggle he was still hopeful of a more or less endurable solution in Pomerania. He knew personally the leader of the pro-Nazi 'German Christians' there, a certain Pastor Thom-Pustamin, who belonged to the Young Lutherans; and he hoped to be able to work with him to some extent. He was soon to be disillusioned.

At the rigged church elections on July 23rd, 1933, the German Christians were victors even in Pomerania. Their leader, Pastor Thom, became 'Bishop', a post that had not existed in Pomerania since the Prussian king had given up the office of 'Supreme Bishop' of his Provincial Church. The 'Working party for a living People's Church' shrank to a tiny group. Thadden still remained a member of the provincial church council, and so was a witness of the incredible things that now happened in Pomerania. For instance, he saw the delegates of the German Christians march into the session of the synod at Stettin in Nazi uniform. During divine service in a Pomeranian church, the Horst-Wessel song was substituted for the usual anthem. A pastor belonging to the German Christians took it upon himself to celebrate Holy Communion in Brownshirt uniform complete with belt and dagger. Bishop Thom assumed, by permission of the Nazi party, the medieval title of 'Bishop of Cammin'. Such things began to arouse protest and resistance. On one occasion a minister extinguished the candles on the altar as his bishop entered the church.

In this intolerable situation Thadden was persuaded by friends in the synod to seek an interview with Thom in order to appeal to his conscience. They talked far into the night; but the situation in the Church remained unchanged.

The first public break occurred at the end of 1933. All the members of the synod were required to swear 'inviolable' loyalty and obedience to their bishop. All the members of the 'Working party for a living People's Church' refused and resigned from the synod.

The same evening Thadden attended a meeting of the 'Working party' which decided to work more or less independently. Inevitably Thadden became their leader. They opened an office in the castle at Stettin and appointed as leader Stephanie von Mackensen, the wife of the acting lord lieutenant of the province of Pomerania and a member of the synod. At first their whole office equipment consisted of one account-book; but this was the beginning of what was to become within a few weeks the Confessional Synod and the Council of Brethren of the Pomeranian Confessional Church.

A few days after withdrawing from the official synod on January 22nd, 1934, Thadden addressed a Church Assembly in Stettin. It was the speech of a deeply moved and indignant man. He did not attack the National Socialist state. On the contrary, he said: 'Hitler's Third Reich has the great merit that the state is at last beginning to become what it has not been hitherto, namely a state. We want the new state. We want the state to be a state.' He defended himself vigorously against the accusation that he wanted to 'hinder the work of unifying the nation', and rejected bitterly the common taunt of being a 'reactionary'. But he went on: 'What has been happening in the Church during the last few weeks we can never regard as right.' He went on to refer to the compulsory formation of a State Church, the appointment of Reichsbishop Ludwig Müller, and the appointment of a state commissioner for the Prussian provincial churches.

So far this could all be regarded as an objective review of the situation. His tone changed when he came to speak of the absorption of the church youth clubs into the Hitler youth organization. He burst out in fierce denunciation of Reich Bishop Müller. 'It is not the fact of the amalgamation of church clubs and Hitler Youth that we object to. What has produced such a profound shock, both at home and abroad, is the fact that the amalgamation has been regarded as equivalent in importance and function to the Church's evangelical work among young people. It is not, however, even that that has raised a cry of horror amongst our German people, but the fact that it is the Reich Bishop personally who has sold the church clubs to the Hitler Youth Movement!'

The final rupture followed quickly. The Provincial Synod was summoned by Bishop Thom to meet at Stettin on 16th March. There was only one item on the agenda, the reconstruction of the synod. That meant the reduction of the membership from 107 to eighteen. Of these eighteen twelve were to be elected by the old synod and six appointed by the bishop. Of the twelve to be elected, nine were to be chosen from the 'German Christians' and three from the former 'Working party for a living People's Church'.

This restrictive election procedure had the sole object of handing over the synod to the German Christians and at the same time to deprive it of all its power. In spite of this the 'Working party' agreed to attend the synod, providing they were allowed to present in a prepared memorandum their objections to the whole proceeding. This Thom refused, so they stayed away, and issued a written protest that by the prohibition of any discussion of the only item on the agenda 'the essence of a Protestant synod has been destroyed and any free and conscientious expression of belief stifled. Quite apart from the technical legal position, these measures represent a violation of the profoundest spirit of the Church of Jesus Christ as revealed to us by Martin Luther.'

Gradually this confessional movement spread from Stettin throughout the entire province. In the towns and villages, in every district, little confessional groups gathered together. On 7th May the first provisional Confessional Synod met at Stettin. Thadden became its Chairman and also leader of the Council of Brethren, which was formed at the same time. He hesitated about accepting the position, because there were already two General Superintendents and a good number of other superintendents in the confessional group. He accepted at the insistence of his friends, and particularly of Pastor Karl Immer, who brought greetings from the Confessional Synod of the Rhineland. Thenceforward he was a sort of 'secret bishop' of the Confessional Church in Pomerania.

The Confessional Church became an underground movement from then onwards. During the next few months, whenever Thadden attended a meeting of the Prussian or the Central Council of Brethren, it often happened that he was passed on from one address to another until he found the council assembled in some private house in a suburb. The members carried innocent letters of invitation from fictitious nephews or nieces. The meetings went on late into the night; and if they lasted several days the place of assembly was changed each day.

In the end it became impossible to escape the notice of the Gestapo. Arrests were frequent. One friend after another disappeared behind prison walls, and at last Thadden's turn came. As a layman, 'a landowner disguised as a churchman', he must have seemed doubly suspicious to the state authorities. A clergyman belonging to the Confessional Church could always plead his official position, but what concern had this layman with all this? Was he not using the Church as a convenient pretext for political disruption? Thadden remarked ruefully to a minister friend at the time 'You have your official position; but nobody believes us laymen that what we do is for Jesus' sake. We are immediately suspected of being convinced political reactionaries.'

Thadden's first arrest was not due to his activities in the Pomeranian Council of Brethren. Of course, he and his fellow workers had been shadowed for years by the Gestapo, and this could on occasion lead to amusing incidents. For example, von Mackensen, the acting lord lieutenant of the province, received an urgent request from the Minister of the Interior to arrange police surveillance for his own wife, Stephanie von Mackensen, Thadden's loyal assistant in the office of the Confessional Church at Stettin.

Thadden had already had his first experience of 'strong arm' tactics. After giving an address at a Confessional Church service in the town church at Güstrow in Mecklenburg, he found himself surrounded by an aggressive group of stormtroopers, and had the greatest difficulty in getting away without violence.

But all this was just by way of preliminary skirmishing. Then, early in 1937, the Gestapo struck at the whole Prussian Council of Brethren, and Thadden was one of the first victims. In the afternoon of 18th June two Gestapo officials in civilian dress appeared at the manor house of Trieglaff. They had been there the day before, but as the proprietor was not at home they pretended that they were dealers who wanted to buy some horses. Now they were back again. Thadden was out in the fields with his loyal agent and administrator, Engelke. Police Sergeant Rindfleisch, who was devoted to him, came riding out on his bicycle to warn him. He had prepared a plan of escape. He wanted to take his chief by unfrequented bypaths to reliable friends beyond the Oder. But Thadden refused to try to avoid the Gestapo. They had already searched his desk, and now, with some hesitation, they handed him the order for his arrest. He was allowed to summon friendly neighbours, and to wait for his eldest sons to come home from a school outing, as his wife was recovering from a serious operation in a Berlin hospital. He was also able to contact the local minister and give instructions to his agent—and even to sign some papers as chief of the local police! Then he was taken to the prison at Stettin.

Thadden's first imprisonment lasted about three weeks. The reports that he was able to send from his cell to his friends and relations sound surprisingly calm and composed. Allowing for the intention of reassuring his relations, these letters indicate that the military discipline of the prison did not worry Thadden much. Indeed, it sometimes seemed as if the period of incarceration provided a welcome pause after the irritating disturbances of the last few years. He was reminded of his lodgings as a schoolboy in the prison cells with the Schläfkes at Greifenberg. One of his prison warders had known and greatly respected his father. Thadden was allowed visitors.

Although his accusation kept referring to 'rebellion against the state', 'attempted treason', and 'conspiracy', the case rested on comparatively harmless evidence. He was supposed to have attended a meeting of a Council of Brethren at which a 'seditious' proclamation to be read from the pulpit was discussed. Thadden had no recollection of it. Probably he was not present when the matter was discussed. The examining judge saw no reason to keep him under arrest and released him. He was conducted to the gate by the prison warders, who congratulated him on his release and said: 'There is a car waiting for you. No doubt your wife has come to meet you.' Then out of the car stepped two dark figures who came up to Thadden, showed their badges and said: 'In the name of the Gestapo, you are under arrest.'

Thadden spent the night in the women's quarters of the Stettin prison, the men's quarters being full. Next morning he was driven to Berlin. His friends were very worried about his second arrest in case he might be shot 'trying to escape' on the way there.

Thadden found he was by no means alone in the Alexanderplatz prison in Berlin. During the exercise periods he saw Rendtorff and Müller-Heiligenstadt, later Bishop of Saxony, and was able to exchange secret greetings with various friends belonging to the Council of Brethren. Rendtorff and the other members of the Council of Brethren had been arrested a few days after Thadden, during a meeting in a locked church in Neukölln.[1] When the Gestapo burst in and seized some of the members in the chancel, Rendtorff began to sing the hymn 'Because it is now evening . . .' and the Chairman pronounced a blessing on the arrested members. Then they were taken to the local police station and from there to the 'Alex'.

In the Alexanderplatz prison Thadden found conditions very different from those under which his comparatively harmless interrogation took place at Stettin. Now he had to live with real

[1] Niemöller managed to escape on that occasion. His time came on 30th July. On the last occasion when he was able to preach in his church in Dahlem on 27th June, 1937, he stood before the altar and prayed for the imprisoned President of the Confessional Synod, Reinold von Thadden-Trieglaff.

criminals. He had to have his fingerprints taken for the criminal records. His New Testament and his little book of Biblical texts were thrown away. He was not a clergyman and so had no need of religious literature. His cell in the 'Alex' was bug-ridden, and he was unable to sleep. He was not allowed to read or write. The prison food, stale bread and thin soup, was uneatable. If his blankets were not correctly folded he was made to practise folding them 'until you do it properly, you dog!' Occasional flashes of humour did not really conceal the profound distress that Thadden's arrest had caused him. At one cross-examination he burst out 'I'm not a scoundrel. I am a Prussian nobleman!'

The new charge brought against him was that he was partly responsible for a circular addressed to students to induce them to join the banned theological seminary of the Confessional Church. That could well be a serious charge. Thadden was still Chairman of the German SCM, and so an object of suspicion as a leader of Christian students. He decided on a counter-attack. Unnoticed by the guard he succeeded in reaching the office of the officer in charge of the Church section of the Gestapo, a certain Chantré, a government official, and descendant of a Huguenot family that had fled to Prussia from France during the religious persecution in the seventeenth century. His father was a church superintendent. For three-quarters of an hour Thadden argued with this 'forbidding and cynical man'. Hard words passed between them. Chantré claimed: 'The times when you could educate students just as you wished are irrevocably gone.' Thadden retorted: 'They are not gone. We shall find ways to fulfil our duty to the students, even if it be in the catacombs.'

In spite of such bitter words, Chantré continued to listen, and for some reason or other was persuaded to drop the charge and have Thadden transferred to the Moabit prison.

Here Thadden and Rendtorff found themselves put into a narrow barbed-wire enclosure, surrounded by the shouts and abuse of prostitutes and thugs and the gruff commands of the guards. Thadden, watching behind that barbed wire, saw in another group of prisoners in the quadrangle other members of the Prussian

Council of Brethren. That made clear to him the wide extent of these arrests.

A few days later Thadden was released. His last interrogation before the examining judge was a mere formality: 'I do not know of any charge against you!' Rendtorff was released with him and they travelled back to Pomerania together. Frau Rendtorff travelled with them, and according to her, 'during the whole journey the two men discussed the question how they had been able to serve Christ during their period of detention in the cells. There was not a single word of complaint.'

Four weeks later Thadden was arrested again by the Gestapo at Trieglaff. Again he was taken to Stettin. This time the examining judge wanted to know whether he had taken part in a meeting of the Prussian Council of Brethren at which the arrest of Niemöller was discussed. He was able to show that on the day in question he was at home at Trieglaff. That evening he was released again.

At no time during or after these arrests did Thadden question whether he had been right to take part in the struggle of the Confessional Church. He knew that it was his duty 'to endure the conflict of the Church for the sake of the Gospel and also of our people'. For that reason he was ready to accept willingly whatever God ordained for him. Yet in spite of his composure, there were times in which the suffering and distress all round him threatened to overwhelm him. When he heard of further arrests in Berlin he burst out: 'Where is all this going to end? God have mercy on our Christianity in Germany!'

Within his own family and his intimate circle of friends he was sure of complete understanding of the difficult and dangerous path he had chosen, but what about the Pomeranian peasants with their traditional patriotism and almost feudal class loyalty? Gossip whispered in the village street and the local bars came to his ears. 'Why does he get mixed up in things that are no concern of his?' 'He'll find he's made a mistake if they put him in prison.' There was no malice or ill will in all this, but just the natural caution and doubts of simple people.

When he was released from prison Thadden had to give a

written promise that he would not leave Trieglaff until his case had been dealt with by the courts, and that he would remain indoors at night. This provided a period of forced inactivity, which he devoted to his estate in a way in which he had not done for years. His friends and neighbours came to him for consultation. In August his case came before a court at last, and he was fined 600 marks. He was no longer obliged to remain at Trieglaff and decided to take a holiday for the first time in years. Then he would be free for the service of the Church.

In his address at Stettin in 1934, in which he had openly charged the Reich Bishop Müller with betraying the church youth organizations, Thadden had provided what was virtually the slogan of the struggle of the Confessional Church, 'To go forth and speak to our people in the language of their sufferings and struggles, and to bring to them God's message, which is the most important thing of all'. That was not a declaration of war, but rather an appeal to the Church. It was a challenge 'to recognize and use this time of awakened consciousness of the nature and task of the Church'. During all these years Thadden emphatically refused to take part in church party politics, although he had often found himself entangled on its fringes. His chief concern was something quite different, that *the Church should be the Church again*, or in the words of a New Year message of the Pomeranian Council of Brethren 'that with our help, under God, a new and vigorous Confessional Church may arise!'

To Thadden this was not just a theory. As was usually the case throughout his life, the theory found immediate practical expression—in this case in the 'Protestant Weeks' movement. As a leading layman of the Confessional Church, Thadden was one of the presidents of this movement. The other was Paul Humburg, the president of the Rhineland Confessional Synod. The initiator, and as general secretary the driving force, was Dr Eberhard Müller, who was still general secretary of the German SCM (and is now leader of the Academy at Bad Boll near Stuttgart).

The constitution of the Protestant Weeks movement shows an

obvious parallel with the German Kirchentag as it is today. Its declared object is 'to bring the message of the Protestant Church, as it is found in the Holy Scriptures, to the people of today'. It sets out to hold annually, if possible, a convention lasting several days, as well as smaller meetings in the various provinces, towns and districts. It emphatically denies any official independence from the Confessional Church and, it aims at serving the Church without being drawn into the controversies of church politics. It aims at strengthening the spiritual life of the Confessional Church, but without excluding those who are not members of that body. It is even prepared to invite speakers who do not belong to the Confessional Church as long as they show 'personal devotion to the work of the Church'. It demands that its pronouncements should be directed to contemporary problems.

The German Protestant Weeks were a real adventure. They were always a race with the police. It was a gamble whether each Week would be tolerated or banned by the Gestapo. At Stuttgart in 1936 Paul Humburg was arrested in the church after divine service and expelled to Baden. At Kassel in 1937 the congregation waited in vain for the advertised speaker, Pastor Johannes Busch, of Witten. He had just been arrested. At Flensburg, Volkmar Herntrich, Professor of Old Testament studies at the seminary at Bethel (and after the war Bishop of Hamburg), succeeded in reaching St Mary's Church in spite of all access being barred by the police, and was only arrested at the end of his sermon. At Bremen, Magdeburg, Nuremberg and elsewhere Protestant Weeks were forbidden 'in the interest of public order and religious peace'. At Darmstadt a Protestant Week led by Pastor Wilhelm Busch of Essen was allowed to open, only to be closed immediately by the police for 'disturbance of religious peace'. At Godesberg Hanns Lilje was forbidden to speak. Nevertheless he took his seat in the hall, started a conversation with his neighbour, a student, and spoke for forty minutes to him raising his voice so that the whole assembly could hear his address as planned, in spite of the presence of the Gestapo. Such instances could be multiplied indefinitely.

In spite of this sort of pressure on the part of the police the

Protestant Weeks soon became amazingly popular. At Leipzig two thousand people attended the opening service, and a second church had to be taken to accommodate them. For the same reason the opening service at Kassel had to be held in four churches at once. At Hamburg about a thousand people attended Bible study groups for four days. At Stettin, in spite of strong opposition from the local Nazi governor, nearly eight hundred people attended the Bible study classes, and at Breslau the Protestant Week attracted a thousand people for four days.

During these years Thadden travelled unceasingly in the service of the Protestant Weeks. In this work he included the SCM more and more. There was a strong personal friendship between himself and Eberhard Müller. The head office of the SCM in Berlin was also the headquarters of the Protestant Weeks movement. The students of the SCM developed a close association with those of the Confessional Church. In previous years Thadden had often regretted that they had not succeeded in developing a co-operation between the SCM and the Church or in achieving a common, corporate basis. Now the opportunity had come.

Soon though, after becoming more and more closely associated with the struggle of the Confessional Church, the German SCM was finally dissolved by Himmler in July 1938, together with its Former Students' Association. Its funds were confiscated and all further activity forbidden. In February 1939 Thadden took leave of the members in a circular, in which he wrote: 'Therefore I exhort you in obedience to the command of God, that you remain firm in your faith, for you are the children of God. Hold fast to your confession of Jesus Christ as Lord. Remain with his Church, obeying his commands. Be diligent in Bible study with new joy and courage. Let the word of God dwell richly among you and work conscientiously to that end. Be faithful to the commands of the Lord who sends his Church into all the world.'

When the Second World War broke out Thadden had already devoted fifteen years to the service of the Church in one official capacity or another. At the same time he had undertaken other honorary positions, but all these linked up in the end with his church work. It was not that he accepted all sorts of offices thoughtlessly. Once in a long letter to Weber in January 1936 he made a detailed list of them, but not with any idea of getting rid of any—indeed, he regarded any abrogation of responsibility as unthinkable. Referring to the SCM he wrote, 'I not only hold a watching brief for what was our joint concern from 1923 till 1925, but I am also the link between it and the Confessional Church.' Of his work in Pomerania he wrote: 'There I am almost indispensable as providing a liaison between the Lutheran province and the spiritual heads of the Reformed Church.' Again, 'in the Central and Provincial Councils of Brethren I am useful as the only layman who can make the voice of the congregation heard among so many parsons'. And so it went on. Thadden only gave up one office. After his arrest he was no longer allowed to hold the position of magistrate, much to the regret of the people of Trieglaff.

During all these years Thadden scarcely ever took a holiday, although he no longer enjoyed such vigorous health. When he returned from an SCM conference, for example, he would find arrears of mail awaiting him as President of the Pomeranian Synod, or a notice of a meeting of the Council of Brethren in Berlin, or an SOS from the office of the Confessional Church at Stettin. Apart from all this, there was the enormous task of managing his estates. Sometimes he would grumble, 'I can't go on like this for ever', only to shrug his shoulders with a smile over his unaltered way of living.

Nevertheless Dr Niemöller, who saw a great deal of him during these years, has said of him: 'Thadden never believed that nothing could be done without him. To me he was always a typical steadfast Pomeranian Junker. He was always there—ready to help, I am convinced, from a sense of duty.'

It is easy to imagine the sacrifice of family life and domestic companionship which all this activity and travel entailed. In the 1920s, when Thadden had been elected Chairman of the German SCM, his wife wrote in a letter: 'Oh, I do hope I am not a hindrance to Reinold in this work.' Her prayers have been abundantly answered. In 1949 Thadden was too heavily involved in the preparation for the Kirchentag at Essen to be able to get home for his wife's birthday. He wrote to her then: 'The fact that in all the twenty-eight years of our married life we have so rarely been able to celebrate your birthday at home with the family is only part of the great store of continuous sacrifice of happiness, joy and companionship which you have contributed to the public life of your husband, to the SCM, to the struggles of the Church and to the ecumenical movement. God bless you for this sacrifice.'

5

HIS HONOUR AS AN OFFICER

In the spring of 1945 the students of Louvain and a large section of the population marched in a torchlight procession to the market-place. The city was celebrating the end of the war and the Allied victory.

The procession was largely in honour of one man, Dr Richard Bruynoghe, the world-famous bacteriologist, professor in the University of Louvain, and mayor of the city during the distressing years of the German occupation. The speeches at the celebration were mainly about him. He was hailed as the 'father of the city' who had brought Louvain more or less unscathed through the storms of war.

Then the turn came for Bruynoghe to speak. He was conscious, he said, that much of the gratitude should be passed on to someone else, a German nobleman. In fact, it was mainly due to the German Commissioner of the city during the Nazi occupation that the eighty thousand citizens of Louvain had come through the war so lightly. The German nobleman to whom he referred was Reinold von Thadden-Trieglaff.

At the beginning of September 1939 Reserve Lieutenant von Thadden (retired) received orders from the Kolberg district command to hold himself ready for military service. He had not been a soldier since the demobilization in 1919, and had deliberately not taken part in the army exercises of the Third Reich. He was nevertheless called up during the campaign in France in 1940, and reported to a mustering depot at Kolberg. It was not at all to his liking, but he was unable to get posted elsewhere. He decided to take his own steps to get his services more usefully employed and wrote to an old friend, Georg von Zitzewitz, who had an important post in Brittany and asked him to apply for him. Zitzewitz did so and Thadden became a sort of agricultural officer in Brittany. He travelled about a lot as far as the Pyrenees and Spain, but his job did not last long. After all, he was a combatant officer and his job could be done by a civil servant. Once again he took action about his transfer. He got to Norway; and then when the Russian campaign began he was put on the quartermaster's staff in North Finland. He found it most unpleasant in the mosquito-ridden and marshy woodland north of the Arctic Circle. He found himself tied to a telephone in a wooden hut that served as an office. More than anything he felt the utter isolation. In France he had come across a captain in a neighbouring section who was holding Bible classes for his men, but here on the staff he could not find any trace of Christian fellowship. He was grieved that not even his Chief of Staff, Colonel Count Heinrich Dohna-Tolksdorf, who had for years been a member of the East Prussian Confessional Synod, felt inclined to talk about their common religious activities.

Thadden did all he could to get away. With the help of friends he was transferred to Belgium as agricultural adviser on the staff of the joint commandant in Belgium and Northern France, General von Falkenhausen. His main job was to encourage agricultural production in this densely populated industrial area, but Falkenhausen had also another purpose in mind. Thadden was to travel about and report to him personally on the feeling in the country and on the conditions under the local commandants, for the general was worried at the increasing influence of the SS in the area under his command. Falkenhausen was no Nazi, and among his intimate friends his motto was 'We have got to think as Europeans here'.

Thadden was now happy. He was able to travel about, and, more important still for him, he had at last an almost independent position. A few months later he was appointed Regional Commissioner for the Louvain district, and he felt that in this position of responsibility he had found the right job. It was by no means an easy one. All over the country there were party spies. Police administration was almost entirely in the hands of the SS. Thadden was ordered to co-operate closely with the Belgian Nazis, and the 'Rexist' Léon Degrelles. He refused, and Rexists who volunteered for the SS he openly called traitors. That did not prevent him from defending a number of misguided Belgian SS men after the war.

He had only one basic principle: *absolute justice to both friend and enemy*. He always consistently refused to take reprisals for acts of sabotage, which were frequent enough in the Louvain area. His office had two entrances, one official and one private. Anyone who wanted to see him on personal or secret business could use the private one. The door was open to everyone. He made many good friends and had no hesitation in accepting invitations from Belgian families.

Thadden was frequently disturbed by strict Nazi instructions to carry out the orders of the Gestapo literally and without evasion. Nevertheless he frequently succeeded in countermanding these orders, and in protecting innocent Belgians from severe punishment. Often he could obtain a contrary decision from General von Falkenhausen.

The University of Louvain is the biggest Catholic University in Belgium, with more than ten thousand students. One day the SS came to the Rector and demanded a complete list of the students in order to select suitable ones for forced labour in Germany. The Rector, Monsignor van Waeyenbergh, refused to give it; and Himmler ordered his arrest. The Regional Commissioner for Louvain was to carry it out. Thadden went alone late at night to the monastery where the Rector lived. He said to him, 'Monsignor, I want your advice. I have orders to arrest you. What shall I do?' Waeyenbergh said, 'Carry out your orders and arrest me.' 'But,' Thadden argued, 'I know quite well that your arrest is unjustified.' Waeyenbergh answered, 'Of course, but you know also that you would be dismissed at once if you failed to carry out the order, and what would happen then? The SS would take over, and all the people in this district would suffer.'

Thadden discussed the details with the Rector. He would

return next day with some military police, and again demand the list of students. The Rector would refuse and would be arrested. Next day it happened exactly like that. Only one thing happened that had not been foreseen. When the black car with the military police and the arrested Rector drove out of the monastery courtyard, Thadden's own car, which had been waiting round the corner with the engine running, set off in pursuit. They drove quickly direct to Brussels; and Thadden went straight to Falkenhausen. He pointed out to him what would happen when the arrest of the highly respected Monsignor became known. The resistance movement would certainly be driven to serious reprisals. Falkenhausen understood. A few weeks later the Rector was taken to a monastery where he spent the rest of the war in safety.

As the German collapse came nearer and nearer, orders from Hitler and Himmler contravened completely the Hague Convention. Instructions came to treat all captured British RAF officers as spies and to shoot them. One day a British plane was forced down near Louvain, and the pilot was taken to Thadden's headquarters. Thadden knew that both his Christian faith and his honour as a German officer forbade him to shoot the man in cold blood. That would be murder.

He ordered the German police officer who had brought in the captive to wait in an outer room. When he was alone with the Englishman, he talked briefly with him and then, pointing to a private entrance to his office which led directly on to the street, said abruptly: "Go and wait in there". The RAF officer went out, found himself in the open air, and naturally vanished. When the German guard came in some time later, Thadden asked him casually whether he had made the prisoner secure. Of course the man protested that he had seen nothing of the man, and in this way he escaped 'by accident'.

Shortly before the end of the war, the officer in charge of the military police brought Thadden an order to shoot thirty hostages who had been held in the Louvain gaol for a long time. Thadden asked the officer to give him a few minutes to think. Then he sent for him again and told him that he would not carry out the order.

His honour as an officer and a nobleman would not allow him to execute innocent people, who had nothing to do with the sabotage incident. The officer said nothing and did nothing. The hostages were not executed.

Thadden remained Regional Commissioner until the end of the German occupation. More than once it seemed likely that he would be recalled. According to a report from his interpreter, Heintz Wagner, on one of such occasions men and women gathered to pray that he might be allowed to stay; and when at last the time came for him to go back to Germany in September 1944, Belgian friends implored him to remain, promising to hide him safely until the English arrived. Thadden refused bluntly: 'You forget that I am a German officer.'

Shortly before the Germans marched out, Thadden sent for the officer in charge of the Commissariat and asked him what he was going to do with all the stores now that the German troops were leaving. The officer replied that according to orders he would have to burn everything that they could not take with them. Thadden forbade him to do so and had all the superfluous stores, coffee, sugar, flour, etc., distributed to the inhabitants of the city in the market-place. He made one condition, that his troops should not be fired on from behind as they marched out. This condition was carried out. Other units had not been so fortunate.

However, the withdrawal was dramatic enough. Thadden held his motorized column ready in a defile near his staff headquarters at Louvain-Heverle. Not until the English armoured cars were in sight did he give the order to start. After the retreat across the Rhine he was acting as Transport Officer in Emmerich. During an air raid on Rees he was involved in a car smash, and taken to hospital badly wounded in the head and neck. For him the war was over.

In May 1946 at a meeting of the World Council of Churches at Geneva, Thadden received a letter from Louvain. Professor Bruynoghe sent him a political testimonial, the like of which was probably never written after the war to any German by a former enemy. At the same time the professor described to him the victory celebrations at which he had attributed to Thadden the credit for preserving the city and its inhabitants.

This letter from Belgium caused amazement amongst the members of the Council. Thadden wrote to Eberhard Müller at the time: 'A case of such friendly and grateful affection towards their former Commissioner on the part of an enemy population at the end of such a war is absolutely unique', and he added: 'I am myself frankly delighted that the seeds of confidence and mutual respect, sown in all modesty and inadequacy, have grown so convincingly in spite of war-psychosis, and the excitement of victory. May God preserve our honour!'

A year later Thadden was able to receive personal evidence of the gratitude of the people of Louvain. When he was visiting prisoner-of-war camps in Belgium on behalf of the World Council of Churches, the city and university of Louvain arranged a reception in his honour, attended by the city dignitaries and also Professor Bruynoghe and Monsignor van Waeyenbergh. And in 1950, when he had to appear as a witness in Brussels at the trial of General von Falkenhausen, M. de Foy, the former town clerk of Louvain, called to see him late at night and brought him greetings from the people.

A few years after the war Thadden was asked by a young officer how he could possibly have worn the uniform of Hitler's army even for a single day, in view of his conviction that 'the Second World War was nothing but a war of aggression on the part of Germany and a crime on the part of the National Socialist government'.

Thadden answered: 'There is not one of us whose actions as a soldier in the war were always completely logical. If we, if I, had always acted logically, we should have ended up on the scaffold as conscientious objectors in the first months of the war. I had no special formula as a German officer in Hitler's army beyond a keen sense of responsibility in each actual situation and a continued realization day by day of the power of the forgiveness of God. You are right in saying that there is no war without guilt, but there is also the truth of the Gospel that there are plenty of opportunities for the Christian in an evil world to live by faith, and to affirm his obedience to the Will of God *in each new actual decision he is called upon to take.*'

6

WAITING FOR THE RUSSIANS

At the beginning of October 1944, Thadden was at home again at Trieglaff. He was still suffering severely from the after effects of his head injury. He recovered very slowly, but as he got better day by day he worried increasingly about what would become of him now. He imagined himself going to his reserve section at Osnabrück in search of a new and suitable job. At the same time he was firmly convinced that his place was now at home in Pomerania. Pomerania was now in the front line, or would soon be so. He decided therefore to apply for his discharge from the army, and on 20th December he finally became Reserve Major (retired).

The Thadden family had already suffered deeply in the war. His two eldest sons, Ernst-Dietrich and Leopold, had been killed at the front; and a third, Bogislav, was to suffer the same fate just at the same time as the Russian army entered Pomerania. In addition, his sister Elizabeth had been tried by the Nazis for high treason and executed at Plötzensee.

From what we know of her, Elizabeth von Thadden must have been very much like her brother. She also was greatly attached to her native countryside. For her also, life was only meaningful if it was full of independent activity. She created by her own efforts the Christian Training Home for girls at Wieblingen near Heidelberg, which still bears her name; and when this was closed during the war and she found a new outlet for her energies in the Red Cross, it seemed a matter of course to her that she should be given the management of a soldiers' home. She, like her brother, was ready to devote herself to the service of others—in her case, to care for and help younger people. For a while she had been content with a humble position as nursing assistant in Berlin, and later in France. Before being transferred to France she used to collect former 'Wieblingen children' round her in the cellar apartment of a friend, and was thus able to help many of them in the difficulties and confusion of war-time. She, like her brother, enjoyed conversation. The most trying aspect of her long months of arrest in solitary confinement was not to have anyone to talk to. She, too, shared the family pride. To be accused of treason to her fatherland filled her with shame and indignation. She, too, was profoundly religious.

Anyone so constituted would be unlikely to come to harm except through their own imprudence or naive trust in others. That was how Elizabeth von Thadden fell blindly into the trap laid for her, a trap so mean as to be beyond her imagination, and before which she, as an upright and honourable woman, had no defence. In 1943 she was working as nursing assistant in a soldiers' convalescent home in France and went on leave to Berlin. One day a friendly-looking young man called on her, bringing a letter from an old friend in Switzerland, asking her to put the young man in touch with Christian people in Berlin. Elizabeth invited him to tea and at the same time the ambassador Kiep and another embassy official van Scherpenberg, later Foreign Secretary in Bonn. They had just heard about the fall of Mussolini and the defection of Italy; and naturally conversation turned on this event. They reckoned that the war was definitely lost, and talked of making contact with sympathetic circles abroad. Then the young man offered to take a letter to Switzerland, and Elizabeth wrote a note to Siegmund-Schultze, whose friendship with the Thaddens went back to the days of social work in Berlin. He had been arrested in 1933; and although he was released after his trial, he was banished to Switzerland. Elizabeth von Thadden had visited him there many times since, and he had been the chairman of the governing body of her school. But this letter, which was intended to make contact with him again in 1943, was handed over to the Gestapo by the young man who was a Nazi spy.

A few weeks later Elizabeth was arrested in France. After an interrogation in Paris lasting twenty-four hours she was sent to the concentration camp at Ravensbrück for further investigation. On the 1st of July she was brought before the People's Court together with other guests at her fateful tea-party. She and Kiep were condemned to death.

Thadden came from Louvain to Berlin to be present at her trial, and was allowed to see her during the recess, together with her sister Ehrengard. She was optimistic and asked them to do what they could to see that she was not handcuffed, for that she could not bear. About an hour later she was led away—in handcuffs.

She had to endure two more months in the cells. Her sister-in-law, Reinold's wife, was able to visit her shortly before her execution. After the abortive attempt on Hitler's life on 20th July there seemed little hope of saving Elizabeth von Thadden. During these weeks she felt 'as if she was slowly leaving her earthly chrysalis', and when she was led out to execution on 8th September she felt a sense of triumph. Her last words before she entered the execution room were: 'Make an end, O Lord, make an end of our misery.'

Even today, Reinold von Thadden does not like to talk about his sister's death. At the time, in October 1944, he wrote in reply to a letter of sympathy from Eberhard Müller: 'I am so shattered, so troubled in mind, that I welcomed your words of consolation as a thirsty man drinks fresh water from a spring.'

Thadden tried to keep the work of the estate at Trieglaff going as long as possible. Every day brought nearer the departure of the hired Russian labourers, who had been working contentedly enough up till then. It had been a matter of great concern to him that there had been a camp of Russian prisoners at Trieglaff. As far as they could he and his wife tried to make their lot easier. When the camp was first opened he went to Greifenberg and got shoes and other clothing from the army stores for the prisoners. In the winter his wife took them gloves. They always got enough to eat, and on one visit to Trieglaff Rendtorff watched a bathing-party of

Russians in the Trieglaff lake. 'I don't suppose that ever happened anywhere else,' he said.

Now the good reputation of the family for kindness had its reward. A few days before the Russian invasion one of the prisoners who said he was a Russian officer came to Thadden with a piece of paper, testifying to the kindness of his 'employer', and this document was of some use to Thadden, at least during the first days of the occupation. Although the battle line was getting nearer every day, Thadden never altered his determination to stay in Trieglaff. 'I have always considered my position as a big landowner as implying a patriarchal responsibility for my people; and now I must keep faith with them.' Indeed, Thadden found that his people clung more and more closely to him, and when it became known that he intended to stay with them they showed their respect by addressing him only as 'Major'. Thadden now regarded himself as their commanding officer. In his last letter to his son Franz-Lorenz in Bavaria, written on 1st March, 1945, he wrote after the printed details of the sender the word 'Major'.

In this letter, written on an odd scrap of paper, he gave his son some most important information. A military transport was taking the historic Bismarck archives to safety, and Thadden was able to send two crates of personal possessions with them to Thuringia, including pictures, books, family records and silver. His youngest son, Rudolf, would stay at Trieglaff, as he did not want to leave his mother and was also not very well. The letter ended: 'The Russians are already at Labes. God have mercy on us and protect you. *Father*.'

During the next few days several Trieglaff families tried to get away in carts. Most of them were back again within a few hours. The roads were already under artillery fire. Thadden forbade his people to go. He had the carts they had prepared driven into the woods.

During the last few weeks Trieglaff rendered a splendid and kindly service that was quite in line with the hospitable traditions of the old manor houses of Pomerania. For a few hours or days it became an island of peace and quiet for the many refugees fleeing from East and West Prussia and from East Pomerania. Just four days before the end a convoy arrived from the East with thirty-five vehicles and more than a hundred people, among them Frau Vera von Korff from Warthegau with her husband and mother.

Vera von Korff described the time they spent at Trieglaff. 'During the last few weeks we have stayed overnight in a number of country houses, but always the increasing disturbance, the coming and going of refugees, the heaps of straw in the beautiful living-rooms, the chaotic piles of furniture and the banging of doors, made real rest impossible. At Trieglaff, however, nothing suggested the nearness of the battlefront. We refugees were treated as guests to be cared for and entertained. I even noticed that the men folk went round to look at the farm and the stables. We were allowed to take up to our bedrooms books out of the library, and in the evening Herr von Thadden showed us his historic collections, interesting documents on the hundred years' history of the property, and some valuable Bismarck mementos.

'Each of the two days we spent at Trieglaff ended with family prayers taken by von Thadden or his wife and attended by the family, the staff, and the refugees. I remember that on the final day the prayers were interrupted by a power cut. They soon found a lamp, however, and the singing of the hymn "Who lets the Lord God have His way" in the semi-darkness was most impressive. We soon heard about Herr von Thadden's decision to remain at Trieglaff and discussed it amongst ourselves. The arrival of the Russians was only a matter of days. Thadden said, "I belong here. Where should I go to?" We felt that behind these simple words lay an unshakable faith in the guidance of God.

'We did our best not to disturb by advice and prophecies these last strange days, in which he and his wife were our really wonderful hosts, in the best sense of the word. On the first evening in Trieglaff we assembled in a big living-room. Then the doors into the dining-room were opened and each of us was shown his or her place at an enormous table as if it were a hunt banquet. Herr von Thadden placed my mother, as the eldest guest, on his right and me on his left. Then to my astonishment he asked me in almost a whisper: "Do you mind if I ask you whether your mother comes from the Ekau family or the Kautzmünde?" As though it were the most obvious thing in the world he mentioned the names of two branches of the family of the Counts Pahlen in the Baltic states, families which had suffered war and revolution, confiscation and destruction for twenty-seven years—but whose names meant for us home and pleasant memories of childhood, because my mother did indeed come from there.

'I must have looked completely bewildered, for I noticed an unmistakable twinkle in my neighbour's eyes. When I stammered out, "How do you know anything about Ekau and Kautzmünde?" Herr von Thadden laughed and said, "Remember that in 1918 when I was with the Dragoons, I got to know your beautiful Baltic country from Courland to Esthonia. Besides, genealogy is a hobby of mine; and a fortnight after we entered Courland your people said that I knew more about the old families there than the Balts themselves." With these few words the ice was broken. We found a hundred points of contact and innumerable mutual acquaintances. This warm, friendly reception at Trieglaff fortified and prepared us for the dreadful weeks to come.'

7

THE CHURCH OF THE DYING

IN the evening of 5th March, a Monday, the Russians arrived. At first there were only a few, and they soon disappeared. Then hordes of them came swarming over the village and the estate. Most of them were drunk. They had found some spirits in the distillery on a neighbouring estate. The night was filled with the sound of the wild misbehaviour of the indisciplined soldiers. A barn went up in flames.

Thadden opened the door to the Russian soldiers himself. Then he and his wife went through the park down to the lake. Behind them they could hear the shouting of the soldiers and the screams of the terrified villagers.

Next morning at dawn the Trieglaff residents met again at the southern end of the lake. Thadden took from a pocket his book of texts and read out the text for the day. 'We are troubled on every side yet not distressed; we are perplexed but not in despair.' Then he conducted family prayers.

His first concern was for the young girls of his household. He first hid them in the potato cellar, and then in the hot-house. Again and again Thadden ventured into the farm and into the village, accompanied by his faithful companion Robert, a French prisoner-of-war, who was horrified at the wanton behaviour of his Russian 'allies'. When a Russian tried to seize one of the women, Robert stood in front of her and said: 'She is my wife!'

On Wednesday they had to leave Trieglaff. Thadden and his family went into the woods to the carts hidden there. Not till

Friday was any sort of order brought into the chaos. Then a Russian colonel made his headquarters in the manor house and appointed Thadden as a sort of civilian commandant. In return Thadden said to the colonel, 'Then you must protect me.' Thadden's family and staff were now permitted to return to the old manor house. They found accommodation in the ironing-room. At night they laid mattresses side by side on the floor. The men slept nearest the door. One night a drunken Russian soldier staggered in. 'All these people in this room are my family,' Thadden told him, to which the soldier replied: 'All these your daughters? What a virile commandant!'

Thadden was able to stay another fortnight in his home. During that time his agent, Engelke, who had been his faithful right-hand man for so many years, and his neighbour and cousin Baron Senfft were both shot. One man after another was led away: on 20th March Thadden's turn came. When he returned with the colonel from riding through the fields a detachment of the secret police was waiting for him. He had to go with them just as he was, and so his tragic journey to the Arctic Circle began. Years later Thadden himself described the journey.

'I was taken first by car to Greifenberg, and went on next day on foot to Plathe. Here a sort of internment camp had been organized on a farm belonging to the Bismarck-Osten estate. It was mild damp spring weather, and the snow was melting in the fields everywhere. We had very little to eat, only warm water with a few potatoes floating in it. The consequence of this inadequate and unhealthy diet was that I soon became ill with dysentery and a high temperature.

'After nine days I was put on a lorry with a lot of fellow sufferers and taken to Landsberg on the Warthe. In this lorry we lay like sardines in two layers with the Russians on the top. In this way we travelled 200 kilometres to Landsberg. Here we were put into a cellar, and the interrogations began. I was questioned nine times always at night. The last interrogation lasted thirteen hours. The questions were concerned with the same points always:

'Who actually are you?'

'How can you say you are not a criminal if you were still a landowner?'

'Where were you a soldier and what did you do as Regional Commissioner of Louvain?'

'How long have you been a member of the Nazi party?'

The Russians simply could not understand how anybody could be at the same time a landowner, an army major and an anti-fascist. In their view one excluded the other. Nor could they begin to understand my activities in the Confessional Church. On that subject their interrogation was always something like this:

Commissar: 'Are you a Pope?'
Thadden: 'No, I am not a clergyman.'
Commissar: 'What are you, then?'
Thadden: 'I am the Chairman of the Confessional Synod of Pomerania.'
Commissar: 'Good. I understand what the Holy Synod is. You are a bishop?'
Thadden: 'No, I am not a bishop, but a lay member of the Church, entrusted with the task of leadership.'
Commissar: 'That is enough. Don't lie to me. Now I know what you are—You are a Patriarch!'

The Russians could not understand at all the resistance of the Confessional Church, and it was particularly unfortunate that the word 'synod' had been mentioned. Synods had associations with the Orthodox Church and were identified in their minds with Czarism and reaction.

'The worst interrogation was the last one. After long and distressing hours of questioning the Commissar made a final attempt to extort an admission from me. He said, "You must have been a Nazi! If you do not admit within five minutes that you joined the party in 1934 at the latest, you will be shot in ten minutes", and he took out his watch. I replied, "Do what you like.

I was never in the Nazi party. I am telling you the truth." Then the Commissar put his watch back into his pocket, took out a large revolver and struck me with the butt. At the same time the interpreter, who was a man this time instead of the usual woman, took his belt and lashed out blindly at me. In spite of this ill-treatment I still admitted nothing. Nevertheless, an entry was made in my papers that I had been a member of the Nazi party. I cannot imagine how I endured all this with a temperature of 104°.

'All this happened on Maundy Thursday 1945. I was then pushed half-dead into a cellar that was already full of people. They had to stand up, for there was no room to sit down. I staggered in. My legs would no longer support me and I was on the point of collapsing, when I heard a voice from the other side of the room. "Come over here. There is a bit of room for you in this corner!" I staggered through to him and found there actually was a little space where I could at least squat down. The man who had called me over to him was elderly. As I squatted beside him I heard him repeating softly to himself the words of the psalm "The Lord is my shepherd, I shall not want". I found out later that he was a devout pietist teacher from Eastern Pomerania.

'From that moment I experienced not only spiritual comfort, but an almost physical re-invigoration; and the amazing but unshakable conviction was born in me that again in this new difficult situation God would not leave me in the lurch. And indeed he did not, neither then nor later, when death raged all round me, and when passed by the Russian camp doctors for release to Germany and eight times crossed off the lists by competent authorities, I had lost all hope of returning home to my people.

'When I woke up the following morning I was lying on a mattress in a larger cellar and running a high temperature. Somebody gave me a pill to swallow. The old man who had spoken to me in the cellar the night before was also there. He said: "Today is Good Friday. Ought we not to hold a little service?" He took from his pocket a little New Testament and read the story of the passion. Then he sang a few verses of a chorale, and some of us did our best to join in. It was indeed a church of the dying.

'Next morning we had to parade outside naked. One or two commissars had a look at us, and possibly there was a doctor among them. Then we had to dress, and I suddenly found my shoes had disappeared. I hunted about for a long time, and at last found an old patent leather shoe that was much too small for me and another old shoe that was much too big. With this footwear I had to march to Schwiebus, about thirty-five miles.

'The youngest marched in front to set the speed and the rest of us crawled along behind. It was made quite clear to us that anybody who dropped out would be shot.

'I managed to drag myself along for about ten miles. My clothes were sticking to me, my feet were sore, and I had a temperature. In one place a cool breeze blowing through a forest lane freshened me up a little. Then just as I felt I was at the end of my strength a text from Isaiah came into my mind: "They that wait upon the Lord shall renew their strength; they shall mount up with wings as eagles; they shall run and not be weary; and they shall walk and not faint." That text kept me going for a while, but I was now at the back of this lamentable procession, being urged on with kicks. Then I could do no more, and collapsed to the ground.

'At this moment a car came by, stopped, and a Russian officer got out. It passed through my fevered brain "He will order you to be shot." Instead of that I suddenly felt myself being picked up, put into the car, and driven rapidly past my crawling companions in the direction of Schwiebus. There is not much doubt that my life had been saved for the first time on this terrible march. I had met with the good Samaritan; and on account of this incident I can never condemn the whole Russian people, or persist in feeling a determined enemy of them.

'At Schwiebus I was immediately put into a sort of sick bay, if a bare room divided by partitions containing one or two plank beds can be so called. I was laid on a wooden board. From this time onwards until the end of my captivity I spent nearly all my time lying feverish on a plank bed.

'On 6th April we were loaded into closed cattle trucks at Schwiebus and began our journey to the East. The floor, which was at first wet and slippery, soon froze; and on this floor I had to lie without covering or protection, delirious with fever. Beside me lay a boy of about seventeen who had been dragged away from an estate in Neumark. He had a horse blanket and rolled himself up in that. I said to him, "Let me come under your blanket." At first he refused, but I persuaded him, "If we both lie under the blanket we can keep each other warm." At last he agreed, and my life was saved for the second time on this journey.

'It was a journey on the brink of death. The cattle trucks were packed full of hungry, thirsty, freezing people. I shall never forget the horrible sight of those who had hanged themselves from the roof of the truck, and I can still see the dying and the dead, whose bodies were simply thrown out into the deep snow beside the railway line. We got practically nothing to eat. When the train stopped several of my comrades jumped out and fetched stinking brown water from the stagnant moorland pools. Of course, they became seriously ill after drinking this horrid brew. I could not overcome my distaste for the brackish water, and so helped myself unconsciously, for I did not drink any, although I was tormented by thirst.

'At last even this journey came to an end. On 19th April we were turned out somewhere in the region of Archangel amongst snow-covered forests and marshes. Two sledges were waiting at the station for the seriously ill. I was not lucky enough to get on to one of them, so I was supposed to plough through the snow on foot for the mile to the camp; but I could no longer do so. Then two splendid fellows, mountain soldiers from Styria, took pity on me. They took my arms and dragged me along to within sight of the camp. Then I collapsed altogether. "I'm done," I said. "Go on by yourselves." The sentries at the gate of the camp saw us, and sent a couple of men out to carry me into the camp. Once again I was put into the sick bay, an empty room in a wooden hut. I was laid on a plank bed and even got a blanket.

'I have never discovered exactly where I was. It was somewhere in the marshes between the spurs of the Urals and the Arctic. The camp, known as Ssengos, had been originally a barracks for forced labour on a new stretch of railway running to Worcuta and on to

Siberia. I was only a short time in the labour section, and was then moved to a hospital section, where I remained for the rest of the time that I was a prisoner. There were between twenty-five and thirty of us. We were looked after by Russian doctors, with the help of one or two German doctors and Red Cross orderlies from amongst the prisoners. There were no medical supplies, apart from some iodine with which my sore feet were painted now and then. We were always hungry. Our only food was thin soup and a little bread.

'There I lay feverish and growing weaker, without the will to live, more and more like so many of my fellow prisoners, who died because they had no resistance left. A Polish companion dragged me out of this lethargy. He came to see me frequently, squatted by my bed and insisted: "You must eat." I answered: "I can't eat", but I did manage to eat a little bread and swallow a few mouthfuls of soup. Then he said: "You mustn't lie here all the time. You must get up." I said: "I can't stand," and yet in the end he got me on my feet. Then he said: "You must get out into the fresh air." I said: "I can't walk", but he got hold of me, held me up, and got me outside the barracks. So it was that my life was saved for the third time, this time by a Pole.'

That was Thadden's report. Countless thousands of German men and women endured similar experiences during the collapse of the Nazi régime. They perished on the miserable journey to Siberia or in the forced labour camps in the measureless Russian wastes. There was nothing unique in Thadden's fate, and the fact that his health was permanently impaired, that his nose, broken by the blows of a Russian soldier, remained deformed, and that his voice never regained its strength after long months of privation—in all these things he was sharing the fate of hundreds of thousands of prisoners and exiles. He was spared nothing. It helped him not at all that the régime that was collapsing in chaos had already exacted its toll from him, and that he had been in Hitler's gaol before the Russians took him prisoner. He, too, had to drink to the dregs the cup that he had not deserved.

Nevertheless Thadden survived the hardship and imprisonment. In the current expression of those days, he 'got away again'. Nobody who knows him will be surprised that he saw in his preservation quite naturally the hand of God, and believed that there was a special purpose in it. In the first news that he was able to send from his Arctic exile he mentioned his conviction that as a result of his experiences he would be able to render special services to his people and to his Church.

There are a number of reports testifying to Thadden's increasing influence with his fellow prisoners. As soon as he had recovered his own confidence, thanks to the help of his Polish fellow sufferer, he began to try to impart something of it to the others. It meant so much to get the captives to forget their misery even for a few minutes, and to stop them from everlastingly grumbling about hunger. An absorbing discussion with an East Prussian farmer about growing potatoes might seem completely unrealistic in this restricted situation, but it was a genuine help in living. The confectioner with whom Thadden discussed his recipe for a cake was helped to forget for a few minutes his disconsolate situation. The actor who after much urging and persuasion recited from memory lines from the plays of Goethe and Schiller was not only encouraged himself, but brought also to his fellow prisoners a few minutes of happy release.

The death-rate in the camp rose steadily. Thadden estimates that, after eight or nine weeks, 30 per cent at the most of those who had travelled with him in the cattle trucks from Schwiebus were still alive. It was the men between forty and fifty who succumbed particularly to exhaustion and depression; but the resistance of the younger ones, the youths and children who had been dragged away from school, gave out appallingly early. The youngster from Neumark, who had shared his horse blanket with Thadden, died after only a few days in the camp. Even the Russian commandant was alarmed. Through the German camp doctor he asked Thadden to try to counteract the general depression by lectures and stories from his own experience. The result was that Thadden gathered small groups round him and told them about his travels in England,

France and America in connection with the World's Student Christian Federation, and the distinguished people he had met.

When Church festivals came round there was a general demand for some sort of service. There was no parson in the camp, no Bible and no hymn-book. The only thing they had was a small book of psalms which a boy from the Black Sea area had managed to smuggle in inside the sole of his boot. He guarded it as a treasure, as a precious reminder of his mother. With nothing but this book of psalms, Thadden undertook to hold services, periods of meditation and prayer. At first only a few attended, but gradually the numbers grew. The women and girls in the camp formed a modest choir and their singing comforted those in the sick bay, who were too ill to leave their beds. It was a peculiar congregation that Thadden gathered round him—Lutherans, people connected with the Reformed Churches and the Free Churches, an Adventist from Bromberg and Old Lutherans from Pomerania. There were also people who for years had had nothing to do with any church. There was an SS leader from Austria and a Nazi official from East Prussia. To Thadden they were 'hungry men and women at God's bountiful table'. He described the meetings as 'life-giving springs in a desert of misery, despair and death'.

Thadden was only allowed to go on holding these meetings for a few months. Then they were forbidden by the Russian commandant. Thadden even had to undergo more interrogations. His devotional meetings had been denounced as 'political conspiracy'. He had good witnesses to prove that the truth was the exact opposite; but nevertheless he had in future to be more careful. It was only possible to meet in quite small groups of four or five in the shade of the barracks during the sweltering hot summer, and they always posted a look-out, but they kept on with their work.

8

WILL ANYONE LISTEN?

On a grey December day in 1945, just before Christmas, two men clambered out of the train at the suburban station of Rummelsburg in Berlin. Nobody was there to meet them, no one bothered about them. They were wearing the unmistakable rags of repatriated prisoners from Russia. One was wearing the weather-worn remains of a German army uniform, the other the filthy remnants of a civilian suit with a greasy grey-green coat over it. They stood still for a moment to fill their lungs with Berlin air. Then they stumbled away across the railway track, over the ruined embankment, past a shattered signal cabin into the nearest street, and then across country in the general direction of Pankow. From the train, which seemed in no hurry to move on, a few tired eyes watched them through the gaps in the boarded-up openings of the goods trucks. Nobody called out 'Good-bye'. Two had left the others and gone off on their own, and that was that.

They had been living for weeks in the same filthy, bug-ridden, dilapidated trucks. They had crouched side by side on the same seats and occasionally stretched their bruised limbs for a few hours on the same filthy floor. They had travelled a thousand miles, or perhaps two or three thousand, along the same railway track. They did not even know exactly where they had come from; from the Urals, perhaps, from the fever-haunted marshes by the Arctic seas, from prison camps, where behind barbed wire whole armies of German men and thousands of German women and children languished and died. They ought to have died, too, but they had come through—just why, they did not know. Now they were being carted back to a homeland which they thought of with fear, anxiety and bitter apprehension.

Their train was scheduled for Magdeburg. Rumour said there was a dispersal camp there from which they would be sent back to their homes, so they wanted to go to Magdeburg, all but these two who were stumbling over the railway track over there.

One of them, Albert Korth, the one with the remains of a uniform, had once had a small ironmonger's shop in Neutomischel near Posen. That seemed an eternity ago, and in no circumstances could he go back there. For the other, too, Reinold von Thadden, Doctor of Law, formerly a landed proprietor in Trieglaff in Pomerania and Major in the Army Reserve, the way to his old home was barred. Like Albert Korth's Neutomischel it was in the hands of the Poles. Ever since the two castaways had drifted into the same railway truck at the nameless station in Russia they had been worrying about where they should go to. Of course, they had had to give some destination. Thadden had given his wife's home, Heilsberg, the little white castle in Franconia. Korth had just said Berlin. But these destinations were given just to fill in the necessary details on the discharge forms. Whether or how they would ever get there, or whether there was any sense in going there at all, they did not know.

Some Russian soldiers were responsible for drawing them even closer together. At Brest-Litowsk the train had to be transferred from the broader Russian gauge to the narrower West European one. That took some time. Then they had to wait for hours for an engine. This trainload of homesick hearts had plenty of time. Thadden and Korth had climbed down on to the platform to stretch their legs a bit.

Some Russian soldiers, obviously half drunk, asked Thadden: 'Where are you going to?'

'Home.'

'Were you a soldier in Russia?'

'No, never.'

If only he had said 'Yes' the soldiers would probably have let him alone. They thought he was lying and chased him off the platform. They pushed him against a truck, threw him on the ground and kicked him with their heavy boots. Korth was able to get away to get help from a Russian officer, but Thadden had already managed to crawl under a truck. Some other comrades came to his assistance and pulled him into a compartment. He was bleeding from mouth and nose and his legs were lacerated; and he did not really recover until the train was crossing the Oder at Frankfurt, when once more the question arose: 'Where shall we go?' When the train stopped at Rummelsburg in Berlin, Korth suddenly said: 'Look, we'll get out here. I have a sister in Pankow. She'll put us up and then we'll see.' So they got out of the train and set out for Pankow.

Korth had to support Thadden until they arrived at the sister's house. Almost the first question he asked was: 'Where does your minister live?' He went to the minister's house, because he could telephone from there, and tried to get in touch with Bishop Dibelius of Berlin. The Bishop was not at home, but all the same Thadden made his way to his house. Frau Dibelius took him in and immediately gave him a shirt and a pair of socks belonging to her husband—unobtainable treasures in those days.

Presently the Bishop came in and then the first friends, among them Martin Fischer, a former secretary of the German SCM. He, too, had thought his former Chairman long since dead. He found him 'a completely emaciated man sitting in an armchair in the corner of Dibelius' office'. Fischer took him to Canon Wendland's house where he found his first home. Fischer had to help Thadden down the steps to the underground railway, for he could not have managed it alone. A few days later he was admitted to the hospital. He was the half-starved skeleton of a man who had once weighed a hundred and eighty pounds and now weighed scarcely ninety, but at last he was safe. The man who had been given up for dead had returned.

At the beginning of 1946 Thadden was still in the Martin Luther Hospital in Berlin-Grunewald. He looked back over a terrible scene of sorrow. He had had to leave his wife and youngest son in Trieglaff to face a still unknown fate. Judging by all available information his next youngest son Bogislav was killed fighting in East Pomerania. Of his former neighbours and friends scarcely one was left. His home was gone and he was an exile from his native province. He himself had become 'so thin and wretched and what is left of my prison crop is grey, but I am slowly recovering'.

His recovery was helped by an unexpected meeting with an old friend from the SCM. One day the door of his little room in the hospital was opened to admit an American officer in uniform, carrying a big parcel under his arm. Thadden looked at him in bewilderment for a moment and then recognized him. It was Francis Pickens Miller, of Virginia, 'the only American of all the 150 million that I really knew well'. This was no chance visit. Bishop Dibelius had told Colonel Miller, who was on the staff of the Military Governor, Lucius D. Clay, about Thadden's return from the prison camp in Russia. Miller set off at once for Grunewald. Formerly Chairman of the World's Student Christian Federation, it seemed to him a miracle to be able to see again in such changed circumstances his old friend, whom he had got to know in 1927 at a conference in Germany, whom he had visited at Trieglaff in 1929, and who had stayed with him at his home in Virginia. He wrote: 'I found Thadden in bed. God alone knows how it was that he was still alive. He was just a skeleton, too weak to walk, and I was afraid that he could not last long.' Miller helped to get him on his feet again. He sent him food (although the American soldiers were strictly forbidden to give any of their rations to the Germans), and a few weeks later he smuggled him out of Berlin.

Years later, when news of Thadden's first Kirchentag reached America, Miller remembered joyfully that meeting in Berlin. In a letter to an American friend in Bonn he described himself jokingly as 'a sort of stepfather of the Kirchentag; for I doubt whether Thadden would have survived to found the Kirchentag, if God in his providence had not transferred me to Berlin in 1945–6. Anyway, I believe that this was the real reason for my transfer.'

In January Thadden had the great joy of being reunited with his wife and youngest son, Rudolf. As long as it was at all possible, Frau von Thadden had tried to remain at Trieglaff, in order to save as much as possible, and clinging to the unrealistic but natural hope that one day the English or the Americans might reach Pomerania and change the situation.

At last she was forced to move into one of the labourers' houses. Here she had to work at the threshing-machine and about the farm. The new masters saw to it that the former lady of the manor was given the heaviest jobs to do in spite of her limited strength, but her work-people always managed to arrange secretly that she should be placed where the work was easier. As there was no longer a minister in Trieglaff, she used to get the congregation together in the church on Sundays. She had to write down beforehand for inspection what she was going to say at the services. Her sister-in-law Helene von Thadden took over the funerals. The death-rate rose rapidly in Trieglaff as elsewhere. The village and estate had 410 inhabitants before the war. In the summer of 1945 refugees increased the number to more than two thousand. Then typhus broke out. At first the dead were buried anywhere more or less at random, until Helene von Thadden arranged for orderly burial in the cemetery. During the two years that she remained there she conducted over two hundred funerals. In peace-time the funeral bell was tolled in Trieglaff only once or twice a year.

Then the Poles arrived. At first there was only a local official under the authority of the Russian commandant, but gradually immigrants from the area of the Bug and Narew began to move in and settled in the farmhouses and the expulsion of the German inhabitants began. Elizabeth von Thadden began to calculate just when she would have to go. She had no proper shoes, and she decided that if she managed anyhow to get hold of a pair she would regard that as a sign that she must go. One night a stranger knocked at the door and asked for food and somewhere to spend the night. Frau von Thadden took him in, and next morning, when he left, he gave her a pair of shoes to show his gratitude. That was her sign. A few days later Frau von Thadden had obtained a travel permit. The hour of departure for her and her son had come.

When she arrived in Berlin after a wearisome journey she was still convinced that her husband was dead. She refused to believe the news that was brought to her by the kind friends with whom she was staying. 'Your husband is alive! Bishop Dibelius says so!' 'Rubbish!' she said. 'I don't believe it.' All the same, she made inquiries, and within a few hours she was in the hospital ward in Glockenstrasse. Her husband was not there, for he had gone for a stroll. When he returned a friendly doctor stopped him in the entrance hall. 'I've got wonderful news for you! Your wife is here!'

A few days later, on 19th January, they celebrated their silver wedding in the hospital with a short thanksgiving service. Martin Fischer conducted the service, and Dr Kurt Scharf (now Chairman of the Synod of the Protestant Church in Germany) administered the Sacrament. In his brief address Fischer ventured on a prophetic conjecture. 'It may be that some day the task may be given to you, my dear Reinold, of reviving the old Kirchentag of the last century, and so bringing together many who used to meet.'

It was not the first time that the question of a Kirchentag, a conference of Protestant Christians under Thadden's leadership, had been discussed during these few days in Berlin. The idea came up very early in Thadden's conversations with his old Berlin friends. Fischer immediately started to spread the idea further afield. Early in January he wrote to Professor Julius Schniewind at Halle. 'I am of the opinion that Thadden should run such conferences, rather as they did in the nineteenth century, in which Christians of all shades of opinion could meet.'

As soon as Thadden began to feel better he had to think about his future. He was not only completely destitute, he had not only lost all his possessions, but he had no job. There was little chance of being able to start again as a farmer anywhere. He never even thought seriously about it. It seemed to him, as he explained to such relatives and friends who had survived, that there were three possibilities open to him—he might apply for a legal appointment in some government department, he might offer his services to the German Evangelical Church that was being reconstituted under the leadership of Bishop D. Wurm, or he might try to find some work in connection with the ecumenical movement through the influence of his old friend Dr Visser 't Hooft, who was now working on the creation of the World Council of Churches in Geneva.

The thing of more immediate urgency was to get away from Berlin. Although he was soon able to find useful activities there, addressing the students in the new theological college in Zehlendorf or forming a political discussion group in Dahlem, he was nevertheless convinced that only in South Germany, in his wife's Franconian home, and in direct contact with such religious leaders as Bishop Wurm in Stuttgart and Niemöller in Frankfurt, would he be able to find a suitable starting-point.

The problem was how to get away from Berlin. Here again Francis Miller was able to help. Even an American colonel could not do much by legal methods. There was no room for Germans in American planes or in military transport. Miller had to resort to stratagem. He concealed the little family in a fully laden military lorry. Thadden himself had to lie underneath a big desk. The trick worked, and they were smuggled through the Russian zone. Then during the night their few carefully hoarded personal possessions were stolen from the lorry, and so they arrived with literally nothing at Heilsberg, the little white castle on the edge of the forest near Brückenau, whose owner, Thadden's brother-in-law Wolf von Thüngen, was killed during the last week of the war.

Thadden stayed nearly two months at Heilsberg. The little castle, which was originally built as a summer residence for the Thüngen family, was in any case crammed to the roof with refugees. The chance came for Thadden to spend a few weeks in Switzerland. The suggestion that he should come for a rest to that country came from Visser 't Hooft. As soon as he heard about Thadden's return, he sent an invitation by Francis Miller to come to Switzerland and recover his health, and to discuss his future plans in peace with his old friends in the ecumenical movement. He wrote: 'A man who comes back in such circumstances is in a special sense a gift of God to his friends. Reinold must be left in no doubt that we are seriously concerned that he should find the place in the Christian world that will best enable him to make his great contribution. . . . We need men like him today more than ever.' The letter contains a hint of the possibility of future employment. 'It is quite possible that I shall be able to suggest something very soon.'

Thadden seized the opportunity. The problem was how, less than a year after the German collapse, he could get across a frontier that was hermetically sealed to all Germans. Even Niemöller had just been refused an entry permit into Switzerland on political grounds. Moreover, Thadden was in a hurry. Once over the frontier he wanted to be in Geneva by the 1st of May, in time for a meeting of the European Council of the WSCF. Visser 't Hooft used all his efforts to get him an entry permit for Switzerland. The Americans were responsible for exit permits, and at first they gave Thadden very little hope. Then he tried the French. In all the intricate confusion of the occupation he had to have a transit permit through the French zone anyway, to get to the Swiss frontier at all. The Protestant Chaplain-General of the French army of occupation helped, and after a vast amount of correspondence and travelling hither and thither both the exit and entry permits were obtained by the end of April 1946.

During these few weeks before his journey to Switzerland Thadden was astonishingly busy. He had never been able to sit still and rest, nor could he do it now. In his sister-in-law's house, which was already overfull anyway, he got together people from the neighbourhood, farmers, labourers and refugees, and told them about his 'experiences as a prisoner in Russia seen from a religious viewpoint'. Often he had an audience of more than a hundred people. Weeks later, when he had been in Switzerland for some time, his sister-in-law would be asked by people in the streets of the surrounding villages of Zeitlofs, Rossbach, or Brückenau: 'When is Herr von Thadden going to talk to us again?'

In March 1946 he attended a meeting of the Central Council of Brethren at Darmstadt. There he met Niemöller and other old comrades from the years of conflict with Hitler. 'The joy of reunion and the exchange of ideas about the past, the present and the future was something we had not experienced for a long time.'

Thadden was particularly anxious to make contact again with Christian students. His main work in pre-war years had been with them, and it was quite natural that he should turn to them again. Here Eberhard Müller was able to help. He had been the last General Secretary of the German SCM and was now the founder-director of the Evangelical Academy at Bad Boll. In April Thadden visited Bad Boll. The best room in the old spa hotel was put at his disposal, and Eberhard Müller ransacked his own wardrobe for his former chief.

From Bad Boll, Thadden went with Müller to the SCM conference at Treysa. It was evident that Thadden was at first regarded by many of those present as a stranger. Nevertheless there was not the least doubt that only one person could take over the chairmanship of the executive council of the SCM, and that was Thadden. The fact that no representatives had been able to come from the Eastern zone weighed on his mind. It was a foretaste of the bitter experiences he would have in later years with the Kirchentag.

The Thadden who crossed the Swiss frontier on 30th April 1946 with his wife (he had left his youngest son with relatives in Heilsberg) was leaving one uncertainty for another. Of course, the majority of Germans would think him extremely fortunate to be able to exchange the hunger, misery and helplessness of Germany for an oasis of order, peace and comfort. He himself could not but feel a measure of relief, but it was relief mingled with anxiety. Would he be able at last to find some effective activity? Nobody could say. The few pounds of luggage that he carried across the frontier represented his entire personal possessions.

His visit to Switzerland was originally planned to last three weeks. It actually lasted almost three years.

The first few days were like an idyll. During the second week Thadden was sitting in the Reformed Church Youth Club at Gwatt in the Bernese Oberland writing to his friend Fischer in Berlin and describing the view of the alpine landscape that lay before him. 'In front of me the whole chain of snow-capped peaks from the Eiger, Mönch and Jungfrau to the Blumlisalp lie bathed in the morning sunshine with their wooded slopes surrounding the glistening Lake of Thun and the green meadows leading down from the steep cliffs above to the valley below.' Thadden was so impressed with the majestic panorama before him that he added a further picture of the 'delightfully situated' holiday home on the southern shore of the Lake of Geneva close to the French frontier, in which he and his wife had been given such a kindly welcome.

Other things, however, were not so idyllic. A few sentences further on Thadden referred to the great anxiety he felt about a distressing hoarseness that had persisted since his return from Russia. At last he had a thorough examination by a specialist in Geneva. To his dismay the doctor discovered a small growth about the size of a pea on the right side of his vocal chords. It had to be removed by operation at once so that it would not become malignant. On 21st May Thadden underwent his first operation on his larynx. During the next few years he had twenty-five.

This sinister malady lay like a dark shadow over his stay in Switzerland. He lived literally from one operation to another. In the place of the single growth that was removed in May, several new ones developed on his vocal chords and began to spread over the larynx. Again and again they had to be cut out. It was always a very painful operation, once with his head hanging down backwards. By November 1947 he had already had ten operations. Then the doctor decided to operate on the larynx from outside in the hope of removing the whole affected area. Fortunately that proved unnecessary, since the doctor first tried radiation treatment, and injected cobra venom. It was the first time cobra venom had been used for this disease. Finally Thadden had to inhale penicillin vapour, only to have another operation after all. After his return to Germany in 1948 he paid another short visit to Geneva and in sixteen days had to have four more operations.

It was terribly exhausting. He was never free from pain. During the radiation treatment he was so exhausted that it was difficult to wake him in the morning, and he often felt as if he would collapse in the street from weariness. After every operation he was forbidden to speak at all for a long time. At the Ecumenical Institute of the

World Council of Churches at Bossey he had to sit silent while his first lecture was read by a Dutchman. For a long time he could only dictate in a whisper for about half an hour at a time. Writing, too, was difficult, as any forward movement of his head pressed on his wounds and caused excruciating pain.

His inability to speak produced increasing loneliness. 'I live like a hermit, like Diogenes,' he wrote to friends in Germany; and beside her silent husband his wife felt almost more alone still. The doctors called these growths on the vocal chords 'papillome', non-malignant tumours, probably a sort of deficiency disease resulting from the frightful privations he had suffered in the Russian prison camp. Secretly Thadden was haunted by the fear that it was cancer of the larynx.[1]

'It is not surprising that this illness has a rather disturbing effect on my state of mind,' Thadden admitted to his friends in Germany. To the shock of the illness was soon added uncertainty about his position in Geneva. There was more in this than the heightened sensitivity of a sick man and his impatience to find a new and responsible job. There seems to have been a twofold misunderstanding from the beginning of his stay in Switzerland.

He had seen the cordial invitation to Switzerland as a definite call to some position of influence, but what Visser 't Hooft was able to offer him at first, a tutorship at Bossey, did not appeal to him. His first reaction, 'That is no use to me; I have no real talent for teaching', was right; and the additional disadvantage of his loss of voice made it impossible to continue as tutor there. The alternative was to join the staff of the World Council of Churches at Geneva, but here another misunderstanding arose. After a good deal of discussion with Visser 't Hooft and Niemöller, Thadden thought he could act rather as an ambassador of the German Evangelical Church to the World Council of Churches. Niemöller, who was about to transfer the Church's foreign relations section from

[1] Thadden has not yet (1962) recovered his normal strength of voice, but the operations have become fewer year by year, and new medical treatments give at least some hope of slowing down, if not stopping completely, the growth of the tumours.

Büdingen (his first refuge after his liberation from a concentration camp) to Frankfurt/Main, put the matter quite differently. 'What we want,' he said, 'is a liaison officer of the ecumenical movement ***in Germany***, and not a German representative in Geneva.'

Thadden felt left in the lurch. He wrote with an understandable touch of bitterness: 'If the German home church does not take its emissary seriously, and does not consider it necessary even to give him an official position, and does not bother to assure him of a modest salary, and leaves it to the private generosity and kindness of foreigners whether and for how long they are willing to continue their charity to the poor fellow, is it any wonder that everybody in the World Council of Churches down to the last typist has got used to taking no notice at all of the "German who cannot talk"? One fine day they will be only too glad to be rid of him.'

These misunderstandings were never completely cleared up during the whole time Thadden was in Switzerland. His position remained extraordinarily vague. Moreover, things were not always easy for a German in Switzerland so soon after the war. For example, the day after his arrival for a meeting of the European Council of the World's Student Christian Federation some of the younger Dutch and Czech secretaries showed mistrust of him. They were not prepared to admit that a German should sit as an equal partner in the conference. There had to be a special session for the discussion of the 'German question', at which Thadden accepted without reservation the war-guilt declaration made by the Protestant Church, before the storm calmed down.

In spite of his ambiguous position in the World Council, Thadden inevitably found himself involved in a critical examination of the problems of the Church in Germany. Uppermost in his mind, however, was his anxiety about his old friends in Germany, the difficulties of the student communities, the theological colleges and the new Evangelical Academies or lay centres. At a time when an exercise-book was a luxury in Germany, it meant a great deal when on one occasion he was able, with the help of the English and American churches, to make available to them five tons of paper and at another time five tons of cellulose. He managed to get extra food for the students of the Academies, and one or two typewriters for the student organizations. Of course, he was not unaware of the unfairness of some of the requests for help and the envious suspicion of some of the people he helped lest one got more than another, or lest the gifts were handled by the wrong church organization. In addition he received requests from a great many people, some of whom he did not know, to write them a testimonial for their 'denazification', and appeals for help from people with a political record who had been released from prison or detention camp. All in all, it was a heavy additional burden for a sick man, who for weeks could only spend a couple of hours or so a day at his desk.

In spite of all this, Thadden did not feel that his abilities were being fully utilized. 'I am a much too active person, with too much aptitude for practical affairs, not to feel completely miserable if I have no opportunity for action, decision and leadership.' This verdict on himself appears frequently in letters written during this period. Then a job was offered him that seemed ideally suited to a man who had been Chairman of the German SCM and organizer of the Protestant Weeks. There were still thousands of German soldiers behind barbed wire in prisoner-of-war camps, miserable, embittered, hopeless and homesick. He was asked to go and talk to them; and this seemed to Thadden like an 'order of the day'. He was able to get Visser 't Hooft to support the plan, and the World Council of Churches made contact with the allied authorities. Soon Thadden had received the necessary invitation and travel permit.

In the autumn of 1946 he visited the prisoner-of-war camps in Italy. In January 1947 he was in Holland and Belgium. In each case he took the opportunity of making contact with local German communities before going out to the camps. In Belgium he sometimes addressed groups of German prisoners-of-war four times in a day. After his return he wrote: 'This sort of spiritual help and mental stimulus for the unfortunate victims of the war is one of the most essential needs.' In the summer of the same year he was in France. At Valbonne, near Avignon, he attended a conference of

German camp chaplains that was financed by the Missouri Synod of the Lutherans in the USA. There were some French Protestants there also.

Most valued and subsequently most effective was Thadden's tour of the prisoner-of-war camps in Egypt and North Africa. The British War Office had given him a pressing invitation to undertake this journey; but the date had to be postponed because another operation had become necessary and then a long convalescence. The whole trip represents a hard struggle against illness.

When he was at last able to go, in February 1948, he found himself involved in an awkward situation. A promise had been given to the ten thousand German soldiers in the desert camps in Cyrenaica and the Suez Canal Zone that they would be released not later than the autumn of 1947. This promise had not been kept. The British were involved in hard fighting in Palestine and needed the German soldiers as a labour force in the supply bases in North Africa and Egypt. The camps were in a state of ferment. The soldiers felt that they had been tricked, and they regarded the English as slave drivers. The vast Camp 380 at the Bitter Lakes, where about a thousand officers were detained, had almost reached the point of open mutiny. Discipline and morale in the camps had sunk to an almost hopeless level. British officers even warned Thadden that he might be beaten up by the embittered soldiers unless he took the right line with them. They had had some experience of 're-education', often laid on by quite unsuitable 'educators', and the result had been the opposite of what was expected—resistance and even open hatred.

Thadden addressed about 25,000 prisoners in the Suez Canal Zone alone, and almost as many in the camps at Cyrenaica, Derna, Benghazi, Tobruk and the complete isolation of remote desert areas. He wrote in his diary: 'These meetings in the camps made a remarkable picture. The front rows were mostly occupied by mechanics, sturdy types without any false modesty or inhibitions. I always began by talking about the difficulties and problems at home and the modest beginnings of recovery from utter chaos. Then I would go on to talk about my own experiences in the camp in the Arctic, and that would soon lead to talk about God. Then their eyes would open and at the end they would come up to shake hands with me.'

The British 'observers' were, however, not always quite so pleased with him. In their view he did not stress sufficiently the reasons why the British High Command had delayed their release. Nevertheless at the Middle East Headquarters he was congratulated on the success of his mission and given the assurance that all the German prisoners would soon be released and sent home. This actually took place in the summer of 1948.

Thadden had still one special mission to carry out in Egypt. The first Assembly of the World Council of Churches was about to meet at Amsterdam. Thadden had been asked to re-establish connection with the ancient Christian churches of the East and try to persuade them to take part in the conference. Feelers had already been put out from Geneva, but now there was a chance that a personal visit might lead to a definite decision. It was Thadden's first contact with the world of the Eastern Churches, which, like the 1,500-years-old Coptic Church, go back directly to post-apostolic days.

The Patriarch of the Greek Orthodox Church at Alexandria, Christophorus II, who was living in Cairo, received him in private audience. The journey to the old grey palace of this prince of the Church was an adventure in itself. He and his companion Christiansen, from the Danish YMCA, lost their way over and over again in the confusion of the narrow streets of the old town. Eventually they had to leave the car and make their way through the noisy streets on foot. They arrived almost an hour late and were ushered into a dark pillared hall by a black-bearded priest who conducted them solemnly into the audience chamber of His Holiness. The ceremonial greetings were interrupted by the entry of servants who offered orange juice and Turkish coffee in little paper-thin cups on silver trays. In the conversation, which was conducted in French, His Holiness showed himself to be well informed. He had already agreed to send a delegation to Amsterdam. None the less he said he very much appreciated the visit and did not forget to give his German guest his particular blessing.

Thadden's reception by the Patriarch Marens of the Coptic Church in Egypt was very similar. He was conducted by a chamberlain in a red fez into the private apartments of the head of the church. Thadden found himself in the presence of 'an incredibly old man with a long white beard, dressed in a long black robe faced with violet silk, and seated on a sort of throne. He looked like Abraham, except that the lively, dark intelligent eyes suggested a certain Oriental business acumen.' This time the conversation was conducted in Arabic through an interpreter. The Patriarch promised to send a delegate to Amsterdam at his own expense, 'but please tell me approximately how much it will cost'. The Coptic Church is reckoned to be anything but poor. Thadden wrote in his diary: 'Very pleased with our success, we said farewell to these places of ancient tradition, where a quite modern decision had just been taken.'

Thadden himself was a delegate to the Amsterdam Assembly. Visser 't Hooft had made it possible, knowing that it would give him great pleasure. It was in Amsterdam itself that Thadden had his big surprise. He was one of the relatively few laymen among the thousand delegates; and yet he, together with Dibelius, Lilje, Niemöller and others, was elected to the Central Committee of the World Council of Churches.[1] He wrote home delightedly, that it meant that he had 'moved into the front rank of the ecumenical movement, which must, of course, have a favourable influence on my future position in Germany'.

His most important experience at Amsterdam was meeting again many old friends from the SCM days. He worked with Section I (on the nature of the Church), which was led by Bishop Lilje. He met again John Mott, the grand old man of the YMCA, who had won the Nobel Peace Prize, and whom he had not seen since 1935. He had a reunion celebration with Francis Pickens Miller and Pierre Maury, now the President of the French Reformed

[1] He served on the Central Committee until the New Delhi Assembly in December 1961.

Church. He sat beside Dr Bell, the Bishop of Chichester. He talked to John Foster Dulles, the future American Secretary of State. The whole human extent of the ecumenical movement lay before him. Sometimes he felt as if he had been thrown into a swimming-pool, from which he could only gradually come up to the surface and regain consciousness. In spite of all these renewed contacts, however, he was able to preserve a sober objectivity. 'The secret history of the Kingdom of God is worked out, I am sure, elsewhere than in these mass meetings.' Nevertheless participation in the Amsterdam Conference represents the crown of his 'ecumenical years'. Here he was able to see in some completeness the real fruit of his years in Switzerland—his close association with world Christendom and his intimate friendship with the most important people in the ecumenical field.

9

MORE THAN TWO HUNDRED THOUSAND

At last Thadden was given a job to do in Germany. He was asked to co-ordinate evangelistic work and various church associations at the new headquarters of the German Evangelical Church—the federation of Protestant Churches which had now been formed. And now at last the pace of his life quickened perceptibly. Between his return from Switzerland and the announcement of the German Kirchentag as a permanent organization in July 1949 there were only eight months.

It was a remarkable church administration that Thadden joined in December 1948. It had been tucked away in Gmünd in Swabia. Hans Asmussen, its first President, had become minister of a church there after he was driven from Altona during the church conflict with the Nazis. There were no administrative buildings. The officials worked in their homes in all parts of the town. They only met twice a day, once in the morning for a short service in St Augustine's Church and again for lunch at midday in the canteen in the parish hall. Very few had their families with them. They lived in lodgings. Thadden, too, was alone again. His wife was living at Heilsberg and their youngest son was at school in Korntal near Stuttgart.

As might be expected, Thadden made himself an efficient member of this organization, though his job was by no means exactly defined. Very soon his extensive travels made his appearance at Gmünd infrequent, and when he was there he felt displaced.

He found little appreciation of the work he was doing, and felt that he was not given sufficient support. If it were not for his family, he thought he would 'give up the service of the Church and become a forester or something like that'.

The Germany in which Thadden started to work was still suffering from the privations produced by the war. The currency had been stabilized a few months previously, and the problem of starvation was slowly being overcome; but there were still hundreds of thousands of homeless and hopeless people in the refugee camps, women and children were still waiting for the return of husbands or fathers from POW camps, and displaced persons and others were desperately looking for new jobs. Allied restrictions on production still hampered the early attempts at economic recovery, and the surviving machine-shops were threatened with dismantling. Administrative power was still in the hands of the Military Governors; but there were faint signs of a revival of German political life. In Bonn a parliamentary council was working out the statutes for the coming West German state.

In these days of tentative political revival, Thadden felt there were already indications of retrograde tendencies in the Evangelical Church, signs of rigidity and inflexibility and leaning towards the past. He began to think it was high time for a conference of lay Christians in Germany 'if the promising beginnings of revival, that were clearly manifest during the decade of resistance to Hitler's new paganism, during the sufferings of the war period, and particularly in the prisoner-of-war camps after the German collapse, were not to become a total loss, to the unthinkable shame of our generation'.

He mentions another reason why a conference of lay Christians seemed to him urgently necessary. It was two years since the provincial churches had joined together into the Evangelical Church in Germany. If this union of churches was to become something more than just a vague possibility of working officially together, it must be cemented together by 'a real experience of Christian fellowship', to use Thadden's own phrase. For that reason he wanted to make possible from time to time a meeting of

Protestant Christians 'beyond the bounds of local congregations, or the provincial churches'.

The first question to arise was whether there were enough people who would attend such a conference. Thadden was under no illusion, admitting 'that the average person of whatever race or calling knows absolutely nothing about the fundamental truths of scriptural ideas, promises and beliefs'. In so far as the German Evangelical Church was concerned, that meant recognizing a development 'which long before the First World War was gradually emptying the churches, and which was leading up to a time in the not very distant future when with the burial of the last old woman from the otherwise empty pews the last memory of a once flourishing religious life would be forgotten'. And from this Thadden drew the inescapable conclusion that 'the real problem, as far as the Evangelical Church was concerned, was the ministers'.

Hence Thadden's appeal to the laymen, but not 'just to provide an audience for eloquent preachers'. He wanted them to come together as 'full members of the Church, as partners, taking their part in discussion of the affairs of the Church, and being taken seriously as real and essential helpers, as bearers of the responsibility of apostleship'. Thadden had no doubt at all that 'if the Church delays any longer making the laymen active in the community, the churches will soon be unable to count them even among its listeners'. And he wrote in 1958: 'The Kirchentag has set itself the task to call Protestant lay Christians to their responsibilities in all sectors of public life and to make them active, particularly in the economic, social and political fields where Christian principles are on trial and where Christian obedience has to stand the test. The layman is anything but some sort of marginal figure on the outskirts of the Church. He is the essential interpreter of the Christian message in the battlefield of the world. Therefore he must be spiritually prepared for open confession of his faith, and for active service in everyday life as well as in the congregation.'

To see in all this only a criticism of the Church would be to misunderstand Thadden. His appeal to the laity is an offer of *service* to the Church. He has never had any idea of gathering the laymen together apart from the Church. On the contrary, it seemed to him that one of the results of the Church conflict against Hitler had been 'the realization that minister and congregation belong together, sharing mutual burdens and cares and difficulties within the Church'. There was no question of setting up a front line in opposition to the clergy, no absurd claim to assert authority for the non-theological layman, no intention to organize a liberal debating society. The aim was rather to help 'a great many people to a clearer understanding of the nature of the Church and to give them the experience of that fellowship with each other, which is the mark of the Church of Christ. What we need in the Church is freedom of personal belief and a firm allegiance to the cause at the same time. For that reason we should give the laymen, particularly the young men, the opportunity to use their gifts actively in the service of the Church of Christ. Then the minister will find an ally in his office such as he has not known for four hundred years.'

The laymen to whom Thadden appealed were 'people who in one way or another have been the victims of the war and its catastrophic aftermath'. They were the exiles, refugees, bombed out, dispossessed and uprooted, 'people whose way of life has been shattered, whose early ideals have been shipwrecked, and who find the fundamental principles of their lives challenged'. Thadden was quite clear that they must be met in their situation, as refugees, as dispossessed, as rootless. It is equally obvious that a Kirchentag which aims at winning these people for the Church must face frankly the questions they ask about Church and State, school and family, economics, politics and daily work.

When Thadden developed these ideas at the beginning of 1949, in countless conversations and in ever-widening circles, he was conscious that his plans were in a great historic tradition. Before the conference at Essen in 1950, he said: 'In the Kirchentag movement I have simply taken up a spiritual inheritance that has accompanied the history of the Evangelical Church since the Reformation.' Moreover, when Thadden returned to Germany at the end of 1948, the revival of the pre-war Protestant Weeks was already planned. Their initiator, Eberhard Müller, was preparing a Protestant Week for the summer of 1949 at Frankfurt. As soon as Thadden heard of his old friend Müller's plans, he offered his support. He had always kept in close touch with the director of the Academy at Bad Boll, and now he concentrated on the plans for Frankfurt. That was to be the beginning of his new work. In February 1949, at the house of Probst Ernst zur Nieden at Offenbach, he called together representatives of the Protestant Men's Work, the student groups and the Academies. Co-ordination of such associations was part of his job anyway. He put his plan before them.

At this stage the President of the Church in Hesse, Martin Niemöller, refused permission for the Protestant Week to be held at Frankfurt. Thadden was deeply hurt. He went once again to see Niemöller, but the President persisted in his refusal. 'You cannot possibly begin in such an unchristian town as Frankfurt. Later, when you have established such weeks, we could perhaps think of Frankfurt.' In a letter to his wife Thadden suggests a further reason may have been that Niemöller did not approve of one of the suggested speakers.

All their efforts seemed to have been in vain; but then the possibility arose of going to Hanover. Bishop Lilje, to whom Thadden had explained his predicament, said he would be willing to welcome the Protestant Week at the end of July. It would be linked with a convention of Christian students, which was planned for the beginning of August anyway.

In April Thadden presented a report on his plans to a meeting of old comrades of the anti-Nazi conflict at Stuttgart. Thadden spoke mainly about a new German Kirchentag movement. The intervening stage of a Protestant Week was in his mind already bypassed. He was no longer concerned with an isolated event, but talked instead about a *permanent* organization of German Protestantism 'free from the official church authorities and yet in real and close co-operation with the Evangelical Church in Germany'. Thadden's words were immediately received with approval on all sides. Only Niemöller remained doubtful. He thought that such an undertaking might eventually be considered, and that Thadden might perhaps be general secretary, but he felt obliged to oppose any fixed and permanent institution under an autonomous committee and with its own president. Then Thadden pressed his plan urgently; and at last Niemöller gave way. Thadden was unanimously appointed 'to organize a German Kirchentag and to obtain the approval of the Council of the German Evangelical Church'.

After a meeting of the Council of Brethren at Stuttgart in April 1949, Thadden considered 'all resistance overcome, as far as could be seen'. He announced: 'The German Kirchentag can start in Hanover as a permanent institution.' Then Lilje objected to the new name of 'Kirchentag', which meant indeed much more than a new name: it meant also a new programme. And so for the Hanover meeting they retained the title 'Protestant Week'. The question of a permanent organization was still left open.

Thadden got to work on the Hanover project with fantastic courage, one might even say light-heartedness. He had only been a few months in Germany and he was almost unknown in Lower Saxony. There was very little time for preparation and he could only be in Hanover occasionally and for only a few hours. He had to travel about looking for helpers. He spoke in the Academies, at an annual conference of Men's Associations, and addressed group after group of theological students.

And yet all the time he was often a silent man. At Stuttgart he had had another operation, and then a few weeks before Hanover yet another at Heidelberg. This was probably the critical operation. Thadden was admitted to Heidelberg hospital with severe laryngitis, a deep-seated ulceration of the throat and a high temperature. They excised twenty tumours from his larynx. Thadden was afraid he would never be able to speak again. Then he had to appear at a Press conference one day, and suddenly found he could speak. It seemed like a miracle to him.

At the beginning of July 1949, three weeks before the beginning of the Protestant Week at Hanover, Thadden and Bishop Lilje attended a meeting of the Central Committee of the World Council of Churches at Chichester, and after that a British student conference at Swanwick, Derbyshire. A few days after these exciting events Lilje celebrated his fiftieth birthday. Thadden wrote an article about it for the diocesan magazine, and did not omit to mention the amusing story going round at the time in Lower Saxony about the prayer offered in the cathedral in Hanover: 'God bless and keep our Provincial Bishop. Thou alone knowest where he is.'

During their stay in England, Lilje was able to poke fun at him in return. Whatever was he thinking of, dawdling about in England, his episcopal friend asked him. Did he by any chance imagine that the Protestant Week would arrange itself? Thadden remained happy and unconcerned. He said that there were so many excellent people in the church at Hanover that nothing could go wrong.

Thadden was, however, under no illusion about the risks attached to the whole venture. 'There was a very strong probability that the whole thing would be a fiasco.' That was how he described the situation just before the Protestant Week in Hanover. Yet his whole plan for the future depended very definitely on the success of this first meeting. He said to his wife: 'If I am defeated at Hanover by the strong forces opposing my ideas of reform, there will be no real point in further striving for a revival in the Church.' In a letter to his friend Rendtorff he wrote: 'If Hanover succeeds, the position that I need will have been created.'

Thadden attained his object at Hanover. On Sunday, 31st July, 1949, at the end of the Protestant Week, the German Evangelical Kirchentag was formally constituted in the Town Hall as a permanent institution of German Protestantism. Thadden was appointed head of the provisional council, and the first official Kirchentag was arranged for Essen the following year.

Although the decision was announced unanimously, a tough struggle had been going on behind the scenes. Thadden was actually by no means the man in the foreground. He was still more or less in the background, only known to a small inner circle. He generously admitted that 'the Protestant Week at Hanover would not have been possible without Lilje. At Hanover Lilje was everything.' Meanwhile Thadden was doing a lot of pushing, constantly talking to one group or another, putting his plans forward and canvassing for his cause.

A few weeks later, in September 1949, the Council of the Evangelical Church in Germany met at Kaiserswerth. The Kirchentag was included on the agenda. Thadden was there to represent his side. The outcome was a great disappointment to him. The Provincial Bishop of Bavaria, Hans Meiser, proposed to refer back the whole matter of the founding of the Kirchentag. Thadden was dismayed. When Bishop Dibelius, their chairman, told him of the opinion of the Council, Thadden said to him: 'The Kirchentag was proclaimed in the presence of thousands of people in Hanover. That cannot be suddenly reversed.' Dibelius tried to minimize to some extent the seriousness of this unwelcome development. 'But, my dear Herr von Thadden, you are, after all, a well-known man in Germany. If you publish this change of plan in the newspapers, that will be the end of the whole thing.' However, the conversation continued; and Dibelius made some concessions. He said that if Thadden was absolutely determined, he could certainly try again. The bishop could the more easily give way, since the President of the Church Council Brunotte, had not recorded the decision about the Kirchentag in the minutes.

Two weeks later Thadden visited Dibelius again in Berlin. This time the bishop definitely encouraged him to go ahead. 'In two years we shall be able to see how the scheme is working, and then the council will consider it again.' In fact, the council never made any pronouncement.

However, objections raised by the stricter Lutherans found support in the disapproval in various quarters of the ecclesiastical hierarchy. Minds accustomed to thinking in terms of church constitutions would inevitably be suspicious of this new Kirchentag. There was no mention of it in the Orders of the Evangelical Church of Germany, which had been approved only two years previously. It was not arranged by the church authorities. It was not a synod. What was it? What effect might this almost 'illegal' assembly of haphazard hordes of laymen have on the churches? Such questions, hesitations and reservations, which were not necessarily malevolent, but were only to be expected from church officials, were not easy to satisfy.

Thadden immediately set seriously to work to tackle these hostile groups, and although he probably never succeeded in completely removing all opposition he did not personally take it to heart. Indeed, it was not until 1954 at the Leipzig Kirchentag that Meiser became really reconciled to the movement. He preached then in the crowded Church of St Thomas, and after the service Thadden came into the vestry to thank him. Some six months later at Munich, Thadden called on the bishop, who had announced his intention of retiring in the following May. In the course of a conversation that lasted several hours the bishop said to Thadden: 'You know how reserved I have been for a long time about the Kirchentag. Now I recognize that the Kirchentag itself has answered all my doubts. As the retiring bishop I earnestly beg you to hold your next Kirchentag within the area of the Bavarian Provincial Church.' The ninth Kirchentag was held in Munich in 1959. Bishop Meiser did not live to see it. He died in 1956.

During the spring and summer of 1950, until the beginning of the Kirchentag at Essen, Thadden's life was more hectic than he really wanted. Once more he was continually travelling, as in the hardest days of the Church's conflict with Hitler. He made speeches and travelled, travelled and made more speeches. Incessantly he developed his ideas, made propaganda for the Kirchentag and invited people to come to Essen. Meanwhile, as he travelled, he formed provincial committees. He collected friends from the SCM, and got them to call people together and even take over the chairmanship of a committee where necessary.

Thadden missed no opportunity to make contacts in influential circles, not for his own social advantage or to get into the top social set in the new West Germany republic, but for the sake of useful contacts. He was like a fisherman casting his net. The fatter the fish that got caught in the meshes the better. For a long time he had been acquainted with the industrialist Heinrich Kost, one of the important men in the Ruhr industry. On 11th June Kost celebrated his sixtieth birthday. About a thousand people came to congratulate him, among them Thadden. He was not there on anybody's behalf, for Held, the President of the Rhineland Synod, was the official representative of the Evangelical Church. But Thadden was there, going from group to group, talking to everybody. He said quite frankly: 'For me it was a welcome opportunity to get to know a lot of new people who may help to make the Kirchentag at Essen a success.'

He had already been to see Hans Böckler, the President of the Trade Union Federation. After a conversation with him lasting three hours, he wrote happily, 'I really got quite fond of the old man, now seventy-five years old.' Böckler made no secret of the fact that he had left the Church when he was a young man. He said he could not give any direct help to the Kirchentag, such as appealing to people to attend, but he regarded Thadden's project as most welcome. A few days before the opening of the Kirchentag students and curates distributed invitation cards to the workmen at the gates of the colliery. Thadden himself, with Immanuel Pack, the Church Superintendent of Essen, visited the managers and works councils. Many of those invited came to the Kirchentag.

Between Hanover and Essen the Kirchentag was a one-man show. Thadden was President, Secretary, Business Manager and Treasurer all rolled into one. He had no equipment, no proper office or permanent telephone. He had no longer anything much to do with the Gmünd offices, which had moved to Hanover anyway. As he was continually moving about, most of the business was dealt with while travelling. Whatever else was needed by way of help was dealt with temporarily through the office of the Protestant Students' Association in Stuttgart. At last he found his first assistant and general secretary in Otto-Heinrich Ehlers. A retired major and former general staff officer, he had previously been helping with work amongst prisoners-of-war. Now he joined Thadden. There was considerable risk for both of them. Thadden could not promise Ehlers security, and Ehlers had no idea how his new chief would be able to pay him.

The Kirchentag was an undertaking without any income of its

own. The Protestant Week at Hanover had ended with a deficit. The Council of the Evangelical Church of Germany agreed to forgo the repayment of a loan of three thousand marks and to continue to pay Thadden's salary. Later they made a grant of five thousand marks for the Kirchentag at Essen, but also cut Thadden's travelling and office expenses. Thadden explained: 'These expenses were no longer the concern of the official Church and were exclusively for the benefit of the lay movement.' So now the Kirchentag must 'chase up some money'. The first large contribution came from America. The Evangelical and Reformed Church, which had already made itself financially responsible for Thadden's stay in Geneva, sent ten thousand marks. With the money Thadden bought a second-hand Mercedes car. The Kirchentag, which then meant himself and Ehlers, should at least be mobile. At Hanover a finance committee for the Kirchentag had already been formed under the chairmanship of Dr Fritz von Waldthausen, a banker and chairman of the board of the Rhine Steelworks.

The Kirchentag remained dependent on voluntary contributions. For each great assembly Thadden had no hesitation in accepting help from the towns and districts in which the Kirchentag was held, nor had he any objection to accepting grants offered by both East and West German governments—although many people reproached him for doing so. Thadden took no notice of these reproaches. He never sold himself and never accepted any strings to financial help. In 1956, when Hegen, Secretary of State in the East German government, asked him how much the Bonn government had made available at Frankfurt for entertaining delegates from the Eastern zone, Thadden replied: 'You know how grateful we were to *your* government for the hundred thousand marks that they placed at our disposal before the Kirchentag at Leipzig.'

At Essen, Thadden had not yet got a local committee to support him and to do the preparatory work, as was to be the case in later Kirchentags. Almost all the work had to be done by the two-man team. At the beginning of February 1950 Ehlers went to stay at Essen, and a few weeks later Thadden followed him. He found accommodation in a little top-floor room in the parish hall at Essen-Bredeney, with furniture borrowed from Frau von Waldthausen. The mayor, Dr Toussaint, put two simple office rooms at his disposal in one of the municipal buildings in Rathenaustrasse. Within the whitewashed walls were just a few tables and wooden chairs. If Thadden and Ehlers wanted to take a visitor into Essen, they first had to see if there was money enough in their cash-box, an old cigarette tin.

Active help soon poured in from the town. Leading municipal officials took over various important sections of the work, accommodation, traffic control, first aid, food supply. The construction of a new sports stadium was speeded up ready for the final assembly. For the sake of simplicity the banking was made from 440,000 cubic yards of building rubble, thus saving time and money; but one single violent rainstorm during the final assembly would have washed the whole thing away.

Professor Bartning, the church architect, undertook the planning for the big rally. In the centre of the rubble stadium he put up a steel cross fifteen yards high. It had formerly stood on the tower of the Melanchthon church in West Essen, until it had fallen in an air raid in 1942. Bartning also thought up the great bell tower at the entrance to the stadium, and hunted out the town belfries. This substitute for the many bells of Essen silenced during the war has been part of every Kirchentag since. The architect would have liked very much to have staged an enormous communion service at the final assembly, setting aside all doctrinal differences—'a return to primitive Christianity', as he told Thadden. Thadden could not agree with him. Bartning was very angry and threatened to leave. In the end he was persuaded to stay.

Before Essen there were no organized leaders of individual study groups. The entire intellectual and spiritual content had to be worked out by Thadden and his little circle of advisers who had been meeting regularly since October 1949. Among these were Heinrich Held, the president of the Rhineland Church, and Dr Gustav Heinemann, who was Minister of the Interior in Adenauer's first cabinet, Professor Rendtorff, Eberhard Müller, and Klaus von

Bismarck, formerly a Pomeranian landowner like Thadden and now in charge of the social department of the Church of Westphalia. All these were old friends of Thadden, and many of them had belonged to the old German SCM.

In the spring of 1950 all these advisers met at Königswinter. They decided on four working groups, on the Church, politics, economics and the family.

Thadden now had a new theological general secretary, Heinrich Giesen. They had known each other since 1933. At that time Giesen was the senior member of the German SCM group in Berlin. After the war they had met again in 1947 at Stuttgart. When Giesen knocked at the door of Thadden's room in the hotel, all he heard from inside was a hoarse whistle. Thadden, who had just had another operation, was not allowed to speak in case the wound in his throat should open again. Giesen was now a students' chaplain in Cologne, but he was thinking of changing over to parish work. He had already been selected for a church at Leverkusen, when he met Thadden again. When Thadden told him about his plans he became most enthusiastic and tremendously keen to take part. His church authorities released him for Essen and he served in the Kirchentag team until the autumn of 1961.[1]

Weeks before the Essen Kirchentag, it was clear that it would be an exceptional event. It soon seemed that they could expect thirty or thirty-five thousand people. At Hanover there had only been between seven and eight thousand. Thadden viewed this enormous undertaking with anything but exuberant confidence. As late as the beginning of August he said in a confidential talk with Eberhard Stammler, the youth chaplain in Stuttgart: 'Dare we risk it? Dare we call all these people together? Have we really any right to do so?' He went over everything again, examining carefully every point. Stammler regards this as 'the most impressive moment, humanly speaking, that I ever shared with Thadden'.

On 22nd August, when the bells began to peal for the Essen

[1] Dr Hans Hermann Walz, who moved to the Kirchentag from the Ecumenical Institute at Bossey in 1954, is now the general secretary.

Kirchentag, Thadden was almost completely exhausted. The day before, after working for twelve hours without even time to eat, he had broken down. 'I can't go on,' he said. 'I have to do everything myself. I am all in.' And twenty-four hours later, when he made his first speech to about three hundred journalists, the difficulties that had made his life so hard in the last few months could still be detected. In complete and utter rejection of all the imputations to which the Kirchentag had been subjected from different quarters, he asserted: 'I have not the slightest intention of founding a lay church in opposition to the existing church with its orders and authorities, nor have I any idea of organizing a lay revolt with the aim of a seizure of power by the laity. Our aim is rather to help the Church from the layman's standpoint, so that it can escape from the ghetto in which it has been so long confined, open wide the doors and windows to the world, and understand its modern missionary task.'

The Kirchentag at Essen was very different from the Protestant Week at Hanover. More than 200,000 attended, and for four days the town, the metropolis of heavy industry in the Ruhr, was dominated by this assembly. The President and the Chancellor of the West German Federal Republic bore public testimony to their high regard for the Kirchentag. The Roman Catholic Church sent fraternal greetings. While the bells rang out over the town and the violet cross on the church banners mingled with national and provincial flags, it was already possible to see the pattern of future Kirchentags, from the Bible study in the morning to the Communion service and the recital of church music in the evening, from the lectures in the study groups to the full discussions in the afternoon, from the women's meeting to the social evening, from the men's rally to the youth festival, from the special meetings for church activities to the exhibitions of ecclesiastical art, from the recitals of poetry and dramatic performances to the final open-air assembly on the Sunday afternoon with an attendance hitherto unknown in the history of the Church. The Kirchentag was at last firmly established.

Among the prominent personalities of world Christendom who

followed the German Kirchentag movement with increasing sympathy was the President of the United Lutheran Church in America, Dr Franklin Clark Fry. Thadden had already met him twice in the summer of 1950 shortly before the Essen Kirchentag, first at a meeting of the Central Committee of the World Council of Churches at Toronto, and then at the installation of Bishop Lilje as Abbot of Loccum in the old Cistercian Abbey near Hanover.

Thadden has recalled 'In Toronto we were given accommodation in a girls' college. There was only one common washing-room. One morning, finding all the basins occupied, I sat down to wait till one was free. Then I saw in the mirror in front of me a man lathering his face. He had caught sight of me also, for he suddenly said, "I hear you want to hold a Kirchentag in Germany. How many people do you expect to get?" I took the question seriously and answered, "About 30,000."

'Weeks later in the crypt of the old abbey at Loccum I suddenly came face to face once again with my American fellow delegate from Toronto. We shook hands, and then he asked, "Do you still believe that 30,000 people will come to the Kirchentag at Essen?" There was a suggestion of banter in his voice. I answered quite confidently, "I think there may well be considerably more. We are reckoning now on 80,000." Fry did not reply. He told me later what he had been thinking: "Now, I feel really sorry for old Thadden. He is just a poor refugee clinging to a straw. His experiences have turned his brain." '

After the Kirchentag at Essen, Fry wrote him a letter containing these words: 'I am ashamed to admit that I was sceptical, when you told me in Toronto and at Hanover about your plans. It seemed to me more like a dream than a practical possibility, and I was tempted to think you were a visionary. What a precious company of dreamers there are in the Bible! It is no disparagement for me to class you with them. Events have shown that my scepticism was nothing but lack of faith. I am proud to be your friend.'

THE GERMAN KIRCHENTAGS

	Participants in the whole Kirchentag	Ecumenical (i.e. foreign) participants	Participants in the Closing Assembly
Essen 1950	25,300	70	200,000
Berlin 1951	91,400	200	270,000
Stuttgart 1952	30,000	700	240,000
Hamburg 1953	40,000	900	250,000
Leipzig 1954	60,100	350	650,000
Frankfurt 1956	60,000	1,700	600,000
Munich 1959	48,500	1,000	350,000
Berlin 1961	41,000	1,100	100,000

10

INTO THE SOVIET ZONE

It was Saturday, 10th July, 1954, in Leipzig. A lively discussion was going on in Study Group 6 of the sixth German Kirchentag. 'I think we are all getting a little overheated,' the leader said soothingly. Yet it was he himself who had put the cat among the pigeons by asking, 'What do you all think that we should do as Christians to promote peace?'

A minister from the DDR (the German Democratic Republic, Germany's Eastern zone) asked a counter-question: 'Why is it that we Christians, whose task it should actually be to work actively for peace, hesitate or refuse to co-operate with the peace movement of the German Democratic Republic?'

Then a working man got up. He also had a question. 'Is it not part of the Christian duty of loving one's neighbour, wife and family, nation and fatherland, to risk one's life resisting aggression? By rejecting rearmament and refusing to join the western alliance do we not leave Germany defenceless against militant powers that aim at our destruction? Can a Christian support that?'

A minister from the Rhineland appealed to his opponents' conscience. 'If you are filled with the peace of Jesus Christ you must say "no" to war. I have expressed that quite frankly in Bonn. On this point the Church has erred again and again. It is wrong, for example, for a clergyman to become a first lieutenant in the reserves. That in itself shows that on this point the Church has some re-thinking to do.'

Another visitor from the West said: 'I have had the opportunity of looking at some of the schoolbooks used here in the East, and I must say that I was horrified to read how youngsters from six years onwards are being brought up in a deliberately created atmosphere of hatred.'

It was Thadden who had to wind up the discussion. He said simply: 'When our ideas about a more beautiful and better political order become bankrupt, that is not the end of the story. We know that it is generally *at that point* that God begins.'

At that moment in the Congress Hall at Leipzig, Thadden's words suddenly lifted the discussion on to a higher plane. Behind the contemporary political disputes which were always coming into the foreground, the Church became visible. The people who had almost reached the point where an unbridgeable gulf divided them, were brought together again under the word of God. There was a pastoral leadership evident in this layman's speech.

After Essen, the Kirchentag became something like a Christian forum for the whole of Germany, a sort of parliament or convention with delegates from both parts of the divided country. It was a platform open to people from East and West, on which could be seen a harmonious community that 'could grasp the hot iron without burning their fingers'.

It is, perhaps, not very surprising that a phenomenon of this sort should be possible on West German soil, either at Hamburg in 1953 or at Frankfurt in 1956, but the fact that the same thing could happen in East and West Berlin in 1951 or at Leipzig in 1954, seems rather like a miracle. It can be partly explained by the particular political situation in these years, when even the government in East Berlin thought it expedient, or at least harmless, to allow such an all-German assembly. In 1951, when Thadden undertook the Berlin venture, any permanent reunion of the Eastern and Western German states was still an open question, while in January 1954, when the decision was taken to hold the Kirchentag in Leipzig, the June revolt of 1953 was still reverberating in the DDR, and among its consequences was some easing of conditions for the people under Soviet control.

Whether this opportunity was really favourable or not, Thadden's personal reaction was to make use of it. He never lost sight of his main purpose. He always wanted a Kirchentag, and he created a Kirchentag. He simply disregarded all political enticements. It never occurred to him to use the meetings for political propaganda. He would not in any way align himself with one side or the other. As he said himself at Leipzig, he 'was not concerned with the affairs of Bonn or of Pankow but only with the affairs of God'. He brought his Kirchentag together; and whatever might be said or done in Berlin or Leipzig, ultimately it was 'holy ground' on which people from East and West were meeting.

Thadden did indeed talk now and then about the 'parapolitical task' of the Kirchentag, but by that he meant no more than the fulfilment of the Church's duty to proclaim her message in this beaten and divided Germany. He meant what he said in the Leipzig Congress Hall, 'When we have done all we can, God begins.' Heinrich Giesen had much the same thing in mind when, speaking at a reception given by the town of Leipzig to the leaders of the Kirchentag, he told the officials of the city—the mayor, the councillors, and their colleagues—to be sure to attend one of the Bible study sessions. 'There you will see people with a Bible on one knee and a notebook on the other. They will take home what they have heard, and they will tell the rest of their church members "This is what we heard and this is what we must do from now on".'

Nevertheless, Thadden crossed the zonal boundary dividing Berlin with some anxiety. In 1951 the Kirchentag was only one year old. Its entire organization consisted of three men—Thadden, Giesen and Ehlers, with an office in two derelict barrack-rooms at Fulda. At Essen there had been a few delegates from congregations in the Eastern Zone; and according to Bishop Dibelius there would have been thousands more if they had only been able to get travel permits.

After Essen, pressure from the Eastern congregations increased. Martin Fischer wrote from Berlin: 'The Kirchentag has no meaning unless it is prepared to venture into dangerous situations.' The mayor of West Berlin, Ernst Reuter, sent an invitation by telegram to hold the Kirchentag in the old capital of Germany. Nevertheless, Thadden still hesitated. He was afraid of putting too heavy a strain on the Kirchentag. Moreover, he felt committed to Stuttgart and the Church of Württemberg, which had already invited the Kirchentag to meet there in 1951. The final decision could only be taken in consultation with his friends in Württemberg. A date was arranged for a discussion, and then Thadden fell ill. Heinrich Giesen and Otto-Heinrich Ehlers had to go to Stuttgart alone. Thadden gave them full authority: 'Do what God tells you to do.'

The discussion went on for two days. Lothar Kreyssig, of Magdeburg in the DDR, strongly urged the choice of Berlin. He was able to persuade Karl Hartenstein, the church leader who was spokesman for Württemberg; and so it was decided unanimously to go to Berlin. Giesen and Ehlers telegraphed to Thadden: 'You said we were to do whatever God told us. We are doing that and going to Berlin.' The telegram still hangs on the wall of the Kirchentag office at Fulda.

A few weeks later, at the beginning of December 1950, while he was at Frankfurt, Thadden received a rather different telegram from Herr Grotewohl, the Prime Minister of East Germany. This invited him to an official discussion with the East German government about the Kirchentag. The appointment was for eleven o'clock in the morning of the following day. Thadden and Giesen drove through the night in thick fog and on icy snow-covered roads to Marienborn on the zonal frontier. The Soviet sentries saluted and did not examine their passes, but they had to leave their own vehicle and go on in a Russian car. They kept their appointment with Grotewohl punctually. The Kirchentag could meet in Berlin.

In a Press conference in February 1951, Thadden energetically defended the decision to go to Berlin, saying: 'We urgently need a Church ready and willing to face the situation of man today—a Church which meets contemporary man with real frankness and careful attention, prepared to take to heart his hopes and his frustrations, his life and his feelings of guilt. The Church today must not confine itself to being a self-sufficient circle of pious people in exclusive congregations; it must be a body of men and women determined to take upon their conscience the great and unsolved problems of our century—man and the machine, man and his economic life, man and the state, man and his fellow men. The Church must boldly tackle the burning question of peace and war, of the rights of the workers and of the future of our children. The Church must do this not merely in an official capacity as an established body, but as a community of faithful people, actively serving one Master. This community must become an army of lay members of the Church, finally abandoning the fatal privacy of their faith, and becoming instead a vanguard carrying the message of the New Testament into the very midst of modern everyday life. They must leave behind them the outdated conceptions of former times and have the courage to be modern, up to date and wide awake. They must be firmly resolved to revise and throw overboard what is not in tune with our time.'

The next Kirchentag was at Stuttgart in 1952. People from the DDR (with a few exceptions) were forbidden to attend. Then came Hamburg in 1953, with ten thousand fortunate guests from Eastern Germany. Through all these years the urgent call for a Kirchentag in the East Zone could not be completely silenced. In the autumn of 1953, still more discussions were held. Apart from Berlin, the only possible centre was Leipzig.

Thadden put out feelers, and the first provisional responses seemed to him reasonably optimistic. Then came a long silence, and the Praesidium (the Presiding Council) of the Kirchentag had to all intents and purposes practically written Leipzig off, when Thadden decided to act on his own. In Hamburg he drew up an announcement with the co-operation of the chief editor of the newspaper *Die Welt*, in which he mentioned the possibility of a Kirchentag being held in Leipzig in 1954. The announcement appeared. A few days later Thadden was overwhelmed with reproaches for having given the impression by his precipitancy of trying to bring pressure on the East German government, which made it impossible for them to agree to a Kirchentag being held in Leipzig. Yet two days later he was able to read to the Council of the German Evangelical Church, meeting in Berlin, a letter from Grotewohl expressing his willingness to negotiate about the Kirchentag in Leipzig.

Thadden was never for a moment in doubt as to the risks he would be running in Leipzig. He was about to enter the territory of the German Democratic Republic for the first time, and with thousands of visitors to be the guest of the East German State. 'Nobody knows how this experiment will turn out,' Thadden admitted, 'but it must be made, *because the Church must not let herself be divided*.'

It is most instructive to see how Thadden dealt with these ventures in Berlin and Leipzig. It was like walking along a mountain ridge between the two German worlds, always in danger of slipping down to right or left; but he never adopted any diplomatic subterfuges, never went in for any tempting deceptions or wangle. He always told both sides quite frankly how far he was prepared to go, and what he would in no circumstances agree to do. In Berlin he refused an American request to allow a Gallup poll among the visitors from the East. At the same time the East Berlin municipal council was only allowed to distribute copies of the map of the city with 'peace' slogans printed on it, when a printed slip was attached to make clear the origin of this propaganda. Thus Thadden walked with astonishing unconcern along the narrow path of neutrality, a truly independent man, with the assurance and freedom of the children of God, a happy man who never lost his composure and sense of humour.

Such was the man who was talking to Adenauer in Bonn a few weeks before the Berlin Kirchentag, and shortly afterwards was having an equally frank discussion with Grotewohl in East Berlin. To the Federal Chancellor he said: 'When we go to East Germany we shall, of course, abide by their rules', and to the head of the East German government he said: 'I am a citizen of Western Germany and bound in loyalty to the Federal Republic.'

Such was the man under whose leadership a miracle became

possible. At the 1951 Kirchentag, a seat below the pulpit in St Mary's Church in East Berlin—a seat a few inches in front of the rest, according to convention—was occupied by Wilhelm Pieck, the President of the German Democratic Republic. The Speaker of the Federal Parliament in Bonn, Dr Hermann Ehlers, sat in the nave.

It was the same at Leipzig. At Thadden's table at lunch were the Speaker of the Federal Parliament, Dr Ehlers, and the Speaker of the East Berlin Lower House, Dr Dieckmann, the Federal Minister, Dr Robert Tillmanns from Bonn, and the East Berlin Minister of Education, Johannes R. Becher, the Secretary of State in the Federal Ministry of Justice, Dr Strauss and the Deputy Prime Minister of the DDR, Dr Nuschke. Admittedly the main topic of conversation at lunch was the weather. (It rained for most of the week, with an English persistence.) But the fact that this lunch took place at all was a marvel to the city.

These discussions and contacts across the trenches of the cold war, however unusual and improbable they might seem, were only on the periphery of the Kirchentag. They are part of the picture of Berlin and Leipzig, but they had no determining influence on it. 'Meeting together' was, of course, a central topic of all the Kirchentags, but it was a reunion of thousands, often across the zonal frontiers. The Kirchentags that enabled ten thousand people from Brandenburg, Saxony, Thuringia and Mecklenburg to go occasionally to Hamburg and Frankfurt, or that gathered together people from East and West in both parts of Berlin, or that took ten thousand citizens of West Germany to Saxony, did something to heal many personal hardships and wounds. In that sense they performed a service to the whole German nation. In that sense a Kirchentag was a 'national event'. But this function of re-uniting Germans—however important it might sometimes seem (and however attractive it may have made the Kirchentag sometimes to some people) was essentially a by-product. The Kirchentag has always remained a church assembly, a meeting of Christians which disregarded *on principle* the division between East and West.

To understand this properly, one needs to look again at the

picture of the Kirchentags at Berlin and Leipzig; the united prayers of 250,000 people in 1951; the quiet communion service in some Leipzig church; the Bible study beside the statue of Stalin in the Soviet pavilion in the grounds of the Leipzig Fair; the singing crowd in the zoo gardens in Berlin in July 1961; the boys and girls in soaked clothing writing notes as they listened to the speakers in one of the bare halls of the Leipzig Fair; the quiet pastoral conversations in a corner of a church; and the singing of 600,000 people under a heavy sky in the Rosenthal arena at Leipzig at the closing service of 1954.

And to understand this achievement properly one must not forget that all this developed from a spontaneous response. The Kirchentag has no neat and tidy organization that can call up people from the congregations of Germany. Reinold von Thadden cannot just press a button so that bishops and church presidents, elders, men and women from the pews, and boys and girls from the youth organizations just appear as if by magic. The Kirchentag is a purely voluntary institution. As Bishop Lilje expressed it at Leipzig, 'There is a sort of upsurge. There is something elemental about it. It is a real community, formed of Christian people who want to be together.'

At the end of the last meeting at Leipzig, when friends and colleagues came to congratulate him, he took them back on to the speaker's platform, pointed to the 600,000 people in front of them in the Rosenthal arena and said, 'Take another look at that. You will never see anything like it again.'

EPILOGUE

STILL A MAN TO BE RECKONED WITH

by Mark Gibbs

'You will never see anything like it again.' There was a grim truth in these words of Thadden in July 1954. If this book was part of the 'lives of the Saints', and if Thadden was that kind of plaster hero, here is the proper time to stop. But the world of the 1960s is not the world of 1954, and Thadden has been too much the Christian layman to avoid the common lot of the German people in recent years. Like all his fellow countrymen, and like so many others in Europe and the whole world, he and his Church have been at the mercy of the grinding, callous, damnable power politics of our time. Giant though he is, he has not been able to stem or steer the storm of political controversy in Germany. At times the Kirchentags have seemed very near bridging the gap between East and West Germany: at times they have simply had to submit to political decrees from East Berlin or Moscow.

Political tensions with the East German authorities came to a head at the Frankfurt Kirchentag in 1956. A considerable number of delegates came from East Germany, among them one or two highly controversial figures, including Dr Otto Nuschke, minister in the East German government. These were bitterly and sometimes tactlessly attacked in some of the sessions. Some political groups undoubtedly made it their business to try to use the Frankfurt meetings for their own purposes; and the political discussion group—a proper and indeed essential part of any Kirchentag programme—produced some rather inept and unworthy statements. Many delegates at the Kirchentag were hardly aware of these tensions at the time; but they produced bitter personal antagonisms for the future.

This became clear when Thadden tried to organize the next Kirchentag in 1957 at Erfurt, in the DDR. After many tedious negotiations, it proved impossible to comply with the conditions laid down by the East German government—although the decision was only made so reluctantly and so late that it proved impossible to arrange any alternative congress for that year, except for some small meetings in Berlin in the autumn. (This did have the great advantage that the Kirchentag staff at last abandoned the nightmare task of having a Kirchentag every year.) There was now increasing tension between the Kirchentag and the East German authorities. Some of the Kirchentag staff were for the first time refused entry visas.

Worse than this, there now became evident a critical group within the West German churches which begun to suggest that the Kirchentag was too 'conservative' and pro-Adenauer in its programmes and policies. This criticism partly centred around the figure of Dr Niemöller, who had found the happenings in Frankfurt not entirely to his liking. As Church-President in the Evangelical Church of Hesse-Nassau he was host to the Kirchentag in this city. He always had some doubts about the Kirchentag, as a permanent organization independent of the church machinery.

Such criticisms were apparent again in 1959, when the Kirchentag went for the first time to Munich, in Bavaria. They became intense and bitter in the last half of 1960, when Thadden and the Kirchentag Praesidium wrestled with the problems of the 1961 congress. The invitations had come from Dortmund (the Evangelical Church of Westphalia), Hanover and Berlin. But already in the autumn of 1960 it became apparent that the political future of Berlin was seriously in doubt; and many were not surprised when the East German authorities flatly refused to co-operate, and announced that they would consider a Kirchentag in the city highly undesirable.

Instead, they suggested Leipzig again. How serious they were in this offer is still not entirely clear; but it was typical of Thadden that he immediately prepared to negotiate with them. This possibility of another Kirchentag in East Germany raised the hopes of many Christians in the DDR; and though many Kirchentag friends were dismayed at the prospect of arranging a congress in Leipzig, and were distinctly worried lest the whole thing might prove another fiasco like the plans for Erfurt in 1957, he was quite convinced in his own mind that any number of risks must be taken if there were any chance of repeating the wonderful days of 1954.

Slowly, as the days and weeks dragged by, Thadden was bitterly disillusioned. In the first place, the East German authorities almost refused to negotiate with him at all; they insisted on working through the East German bishops and church officials. And this was no matter of mere precedence: this was an oblique attack on the independence and lay character of the Kirchentag. Then there came trouble over the programme and the main speakers. The East German government refused to allow four speakers, who, it claimed, were 'NATO churchmen' and in favour of atom wars and West German rearmament. These included Bishop Dibelius and Bishop Lilje.

After long and agonizing debates, not only within the Kirchentag Praesidium but also in the Synod of the Evangelical Churches in Germany, it was decided that the Kirchentag could not accept this censorship of its programme. There was immediately serious criticism of this decision. Dr Niemöller even went to the length of touring East Germany during the week of the Kirchentag. His speeches, inevitably misreported and distorted by the East German Press, dismayed many German church people. Attempts at reconciliation between him and the Kirchentag authorities had, however, already begun when he met with his distressing car accident in Denmark in August 1961.

Anyway, the decision was made; and Thadden has stressed the fact that the insistence on the removal of the 'NATO men' from the programme was not by any means the only condition which the East German authorities were likely to make. There was, indeed, a very real fear that they would have stepped up their demands as the congress date approached. That had happened in 1957. He was much fortified in his decision by the fact that Dr Scharf, the new president of the Council of the Evangelical Church in Germany, and himself an East-Berliner, agreed with this decision, and remained chairman of the Berlin Preparatory Committee for 1961. And, by and large, the bulk of the German congregations also approved: for example, Niemöller's own Church of Hesse-Nassau sent a large contingent to Berlin.

The official attitude of the Kirchentag in this controversy was well summed up in a statement issued by the Ecumenical Committee in May 1961, which read as follows.

'Everybody knows that there has been some controversy about where the next Kirchentag is to be held—whether it should be Berlin or Leipzig. This is inevitable.

'What is much more serious is the suggestion now being made—particularly in some church circles outside Germany—that our Kirchentag organization and programme are, to a large extent, dominated by certain right-wing political opinions; and that those who do not share such opinions have no place in our next meeting at Berlin. This suggestion is completely false; and it is entirely contrary to the whole spirit of a Kirchentag. The Kirchentag is a great gathering of Christians of every variety of political and social beliefs. Like the Church herself, it is made up of all kinds of people with all kinds of opinions about both home and international affairs. In point of fact, we particularly wish to have at Berlin in 1961 a wide and varied representation from both Eastern and Western churches, visitors who will contribute their own opinions in the many formal and informal discussions of the week.

'Indeed, if all those who feel somewhat critical about the German churches, or about the Kirchentag—or about Adenauer or Ulbricht or Kennedy or Kruschev or anyone else—stay away from our Berlin meetings, they will do great damage to our Kirchentag and the great experiment in lay training which it stands for. A Kirchentag is a frank and friendly encounter between Christians, and between Christians and other men and women of good will: it is not in any sense either politically or ecclesiastically a "party rally".'

It was one thing to decide to go to Berlin, it was another matter to achieve a Kirchentag there. The Berlin committee went on planning an 'all-Berlin' Kirchentag, including meetings, discussions and even an Ecumenical Centre for foreign visitors in 'Democratic Berlin' (the Soviet sector): but nobody knew whether these events could be held. They arranged for hospitality on the usual vast scale. Forty thousand visitors were to be welcomed, many of them in East Berlin homes: but nobody knew whether entry from East Germany or even from the West would be unhampered. And the political winds were blowing harder from both Moscow and Washington. Would foreign visitors risk the journey, and would the soldiers stay in their barracks through July 1961?

In the event, Berlin 1961 passed with almost unbelievable calm and smoothness. The official events in East Berlin were forbidden at the last minute by police order; but an extraordinary number of church services (held, as it happened, on exactly the same texts and themes as some of the Kirchentag meetings) took place without incident or interference. Forty-one thousand registered officially as participants, mostly from West Berlin and Western Germany: a large number of others attended daily without official registration. As an extra blessing, the most important *Arbeitsgruppe*, or working group, turned out not to be the one on politics at all, but the one on Jews and Christians—which justified the whole procedure of a Kirchentag in a way which delighted Thadden's heart. Here were Christians and Jews working out a way of reconciliation, in Germany, in the year of the Eichmann trial.

The theme of Berlin 1961 was *Ich bin bei Euch* ('I am with you'). It is a word of hope; and it was taken seriously and grimly to heart. Thousands watched Dr Scharf standing alone in the Olympic Stadium at the closing ceremony, and millions more followed the service on their TV sets. Their spirits were firm but hardly gay as they wondered about the future of Germany and the world. It was originally planned that the last Sunday of the Kirchentag should be Sunday, 13th August—Thadden's seventieth birthday. Providentially, the date was moved to July—it was a matter of the school holidays in the city. For it was the 13th August that the East Berlin authorities built their 'Chinese wall', to ban all access to the West from the DDR. And a few days later Dr Scharf, an East Berlin citizen, who went to West Berlin to see his wife, was refused permission to return to his office and his work. There was to be a new and bitter chapter in the history of the German people and of the Kirchentag.

There have been other problems besides political ones since 1954. By 1956 or 1959 the Kirchentag had become more than a trifle set in its ways, and it seemed to some people rather too thoroughly organized, too much the same from year to year. One trouble has been that the permanent staff in the Kirchentag headquarters at Fulda is ridiculously small, for financial reasons. The giant and superb temporary organization for each congress is largely voluntary labour, which vanishes as quickly as it can afterwards. There is an inevitable tendency to copy the successful plans of the past, and the attempts at fundamental reassessment of the Kirchentag movement, such as the Kirchentag Congress held in Hamburg in April 1958, have not been wholly successful.

Fortunately the success of the Kirchentags never went to Thadden's head, even though by 1954 he was, of course, a famous world figure, lionized wherever he went by churches all too often lacking such lay leaders themselves. The critical faculty has always been strong in him; and there are moments when his own judgements seem much more merciless than any criticism that comes from outside. He once told a visitor to Fulda: 'Here we are living in an empty room. If we ask the church leaders what they think of the Kirchentag they say that the way we bring all those people together is wonderful. If we ask them what the Kirchentag means in the daily life of their churches they say it actually means nothing! Maybe they are right.

'We are often asked by American visitors, "What you are doing is wonderful, but how does the Kirchentag affect the community as a whole? What happens to people when they go home? What about the *results*?" And I can only say, "I don't know".'

Thadden has been particularly sharp about the weaknesses of lay leadership in the Kirchentag and in the German churches as a whole. He is very sensitive on this point: he has often felt himself ignored as a layman while the clerical hierarchy decide the future of the Church in Germany. It is clear that the Kirchentag is both a great church rally, and also a fine instrument for Christian instruction: it is not sufficiently a centre for Christian discussion and lay training. Here, of course, the problems of numbers are most serious. There are not many lay Christians in Germany (or in any country) with the expertise and the speaking ability to address an *Arbeitsgruppe* of 5,000. It is exceedingly desirable to allow the Kirchentag to split up into informal groups of twenty or thirty people, but this is a gigantic problem when 40,000 participants will then need 2,000 groups. But Thadden is not satisfied; and plans for the Dortmund Kirchentag in 1962 include both a radical reconstruction of the traditional Kirchentag programme and some experiments with smaller groups.

Since Leipzig, then, the years have been rugged and confused. One development, though, has given Thadden much pleasure—the emergence of the Kirchentag as a major ecumenical event. Even at Essen in 1950 Dr Visser 't Hooft and other friends from the World Council of Churches were there to back him in this new experiment. Ever since then the Kirchentag has benefited enormously from the criticisms and friendship of a number of prominent 'ecumaniacs'. Each congress has seen major speakers from churches outside Germany; and both Kirchentag and the whole Church of God have helped each other in this way.

Thadden has always spread the Kirchentag gospel in his world tours. In 1954 while bathing at Evanston an observer saw him standing knee-deep in the waters of Lake Michigan talking enthusiastically to a Christian friend about the Kirchentag, regardless of the broiling sun. By the evening he was terribly sunburned and could hardly speak. One of his closest colleagues has said of him, 'If I start to talk to him about cockchafers, in three words he has got round to the Kirchentag.'

No one imagines that the Kirchentag can be copied automatically in any other country, but Thadden has watched with very great pleasure the developments of various experiments in other countries. He sent a personal representative to the first Kirk Week in Aberdeen in 1957, and travelled himself to the first Rassemblement Protestant in Strasbourg in 1956 and the first regional Swiss Kirchentag at Tramelau in 1960.

The increasing number of foreign visitors to the German Kirchentag posed its own problems. Some of them felt lost in the great mass of participants, and were reluctant to sit passively in the lecture meetings. Some of them found it difficult to make real contact with German Christians, and complained: 'We are not here just to be photographed.' Largely under the initiative of Dr Franklin H. Littell, then director of the Franz Lieber Haus in Bad Godesberg, a special Kirchentag Ecumenical Committee was established, and from Frankfurt 1956 onwards there has been a special programme for foreign visitors, in which Thadden has always taken the greatest possible interest.

This programme proved of great importance at Berlin in 1961. No fewer than 1,100 foreign visitors registered at a special Ecumenical Centre, and were able to make very many personal contacts with both East and West Berliners. And since such a number is not too unwieldy, it did prove possible to organize these visitors in small discussion groups—with about the same number of Germans—which has proved a useful precedent for the future.

Thadden, in 1962, is still a man to be reckoned with. His voice sometimes lets him down (he had some more operations last year) and at times he looks his seventy years. But there is plenty of fight left in the man yet; and what is even more important, plenty of radicalism and critical thinking. Thadden knows what the vocation of a Christian layman is. He has known it ever since the crisis over the duel in 1914, ever since the social work in Berlin in the 1920s. He knows it in his bones and in all the weary miles of travelling from Fulda to the ends of Germany and back again. The Church of Jesus Christ, the World Council of Churches, the churches in Germany, in Britain, in the United States—we still have not learnt this lesson of our true vocation. He will go on to the end of his life teaching us, and it is fitting that this biography should end with his own words.

'Nobody knows whether the Kirchentag will survive. It depends solely on God's sovereign and majestic will whether he wishes to use this instrument of his any further, or not. But, as long as he gives us the chance to be obedient to his will, we shall shoulder the responsibility for this service to him.'